A Dickens
of a Cat

A Dickens
of a Cat

and Other Stories *of* the Cats We Love

Edited by Callie Smith Grant

Revell
Grand Rapids, Michigan

Published by Fleming H. Revell
a division of Baker Publishing Group
P.O. Box 6287, Grand Rapids, MI 49516-6287

Printed in the United States of America

Library of Congress Cataloging-in-Publication Data
A Dickens of a cat : and other stories of the cats we love / [compiled by] Callie Smith Grant.
    p.   cm.
  Includes bibliographical references.
  ISBN 10: 0-8007-5846-3 (pbk.)
  ISBN 978-0-8007-5846-2 (pbk.)
    1. Cat owners. 2. Cats—Religious aspects—Christianity. I. Grant, Callie Smith.
BV4596.A54.D53 2007
242′.68—dc22   2007021599

To the memory of my mother

who loved kittens and cats

and was known in my home

as Cat-Grandma

 # Contents

Foreword

H. Norman Wright

Can you imagine your life without a cat? Not if you're reading this book. Now and then you will find a book that's difficult to put down. And this is one of them. The stories cover a wide spectrum. Memories of your own cat history will surely be activated. At times you will find yourself smiling or even laughing as you connect with a story. You'll remember the sounds of a purr or a hiss or a quiet meow. You'll remember long-lost images of your cat climbing up the drapes or hiding in the shower or stealing that piece of fish from the counter. You might even remember the panic you felt when you couldn't find your cat for a few hours, or even several days. And you might remember the feel of that dead mouse under your foot, which was really a gift from your proud hunter.

This book is both inspirational as well as informative. The various contributors create pictures in your mind so you feel as though you are right there. You might plan to read "just one story," but you'll have difficulty stopping.

This is the kind of book that won't stay on your shelf, but you'll want to say to other cat lovers, "Here—you will really enjoy these stories . . . but I want my book back when you're through."

Introduction

Callie Smith Grant

I was on a mission.

I love cats, always have. I consider them some of God's best engineering. So compiling a book of cat stories sounded like a delightful task for me, and I put out the call for stories.

Anyone who has a cat certainly has a story, and those stories are as varied as the coats on cats. I wanted not only a variety of stories but specifically stories that showed the importance of cats in the grand scheme of one's life. Stories that showed cats being and doing what they were put on earth to be and do. Stories that showed cats showing up when needed. Stories that showed that perhaps the Creator sent just the right beast for the right situation at the right time. I received scores of stories that were testament to these very things.

Then I got on a more difficult mission. What if I could find stories that showed cats actually saving lives? I've heard of them waking up people when there's a fire or a gas leak. Those stories must be out there. Certainly dogs save lives. We've all seen footage of dogs pulling people out of fires, swimming them out of floodwaters, or fiercely guarding their beloved humans from harm. Surely there must be a cat out there that saved a life.

There is indeed. There are many, and some of them are in this book. But they didn't haul anyone from a burning building—nothing so overt as that. These lifesaving cats were much more . . . let's say . . . *catlike* about saving lives of humans.

In these pages, you'll meet cats that soothed childhood hurts, promoted peace in the household, protected children, assured troubled humans, and even, in their own ways, impacted journeys of faith. A God-sent cat did "save" humans in the ways cats operate—quietly, low to the ground, on tiptoe, purring all the way.

Joy Davidman, the wife of C. S. Lewis, found great solace in cats. In her writing, she alludes to poet Francis Thompson who suggests in "The Hound of Heaven" that God pursues us like a great hound. Joy Davidman wrote that with her, "God was more like a cat. He had been stalking me for a very long time, waiting for his moment, he crept nearer so silently that I never knew he was there. Then, all at once, he sprang."[1]

Cats have their ways. Felines are on this earth to be what they are. Sometimes those unique ways of the cat come into our lives and help us. In these pages, you'll meet such marvelous cats and their humans, read their stories, and ponder this amazing beast created on the fifth day.

A Dickens of a Cat

Gwen Ellis

Gwen, I think it's ovarian cancer, and I think it's spread everywhere. I'm so sorry." These were the grim words of my surgeon in late October. "Go home, get your affairs in order, and we'll operate as soon as we can."

I had surgery in mid-November and learned that I, indeed, had an aggressive form of ovarian cancer. Then there were complications—intestinal blockage—and ten days in the hospital.

I was weary of being in the hospital. I was frightened about my future. I worried if I was even going to have a future. I had been divorced a year earlier and I wondered how I was going to cope with chemotherapy, my job as an editor, and taking care of my house in the country all by myself.

Sometime during those ten days, my daughter began to say, "Mom, I don't want you to be alone. I think you need a pet."

"Oh, Wendy, how could I take care of a pet? I'm so weak I can hardly take care of me."

"What about a cat? Cats don't require much care."

"I'm a dog person," I answered with my "and that's final" tone. But one night after my concerned daughter had gone for the evening, I began to think about what she'd said. We were so focused on my cancer and whether I'd live or die that we thought of little else. Perhaps a pet would give me something else to think about. Pets have always made me happy. In fact, I'm positively silly about my pets. The doctor had already told me that the very best therapy was going to be a positive attitude.

I went to sleep that night thinking about the kind of pet I might want. In the morning when Wendy came I shocked her by saying, "All right, I've decided I want a cat. I want you to go to the animal shelter and get me a black-and-white tuxedo cat. Since I'm a book editor, I think I should have a very literary-looking cat, don't you? His name will be Charles Dickens. Make sure he looks the part. He should have a bib and white mittens and socks, and a mustache would be good."

She didn't make it to the shelter that day because after all those long tiresome days, I was suddenly dismissed from the hospital. But the next afternoon, Wendy got a "mommy sitter" and then went to get my cat. I could hardly wait for her to get home. When the garage door opened, Judy, my "sitter," jumped up to see what Wendy had brought.

It was a young, bright-eyed black cat with a white bib, the compulsory white mittens and socks, and a one-sided mustache. I couldn't believe it. I had told Wendy what I wanted, but I never dreamed she would find the exact cat I'd described. "Hello, Charles Dickens," I said. He said, "Meow."

Dickens had a history. He had been a very frightened stray who went in a rainstorm to a house where he couldn't stay because there were already three cats living there. The lady of the house wept as she took

I'll Take the House Salad, Please

Here's a treat for indoor cats. Buy a bag of oat seeds from a feed store or a nursery—oats are very cheap. Plant a handful of seeds in a pot with moist soil and keep covered until sprouting occurs. Water occasionally—out of cat's reach for the surprise factor—until the grass is nice and tall. Then spritz with water, serve up to a happy cat, and let the noshing begin. Water when needed. Grass will wither after a few days. Then dump it and start the process again.

Or, as long as you have a lawn that is not chemically treated, you can pull grass for your cat's greens. Look for the greenest and thickest patch. Serve it up fresh on a plate and watch kitty chow down. Toss out whatever your beast doesn't eat right away. One cat lover reports on the first time she offered this green salad to her excited house cats: "It was like serving chocolate at a PMS convention."

him to the pound and told the attendants, "Make sure whoever gets him calls me."

That evening I called her, and she told me, "I'm about to have a baby, and I already have three cats. I couldn't keep him, but I just loved him. I prayed God would send him to someone who needed him and would really love him."

I realized in that moment that Dickens had not come to me by chance. "Your prayers have been answered," I said. I told her my story and ended with, "I need him."

All that first day and the next, Dickens went over my house with a "fine-toothed nose." He poked into every crevice and cranny. Then he began to sneeze. He sneezed and sneezed and sneezed. His nose was running and his eyes were dull. Dickens was sick. Wendy took him to the vet.

"Is he going to die?" I asked when she brought him home.

"The vet doesn't think so. He thinks Dickens is old enough and strong enough to survive. He gave me some antibiotics that we'll start him on right now."

Poor Dickens. He was very sick. He lay on the foot of my bed on a hot water bottle for days. It had been my intention to refocus our attention on something besides my illness and upcoming chemotherapy, and I surely did it. All we could think about was whether Dickens would live or die.

One day, after about eight days, there was a turning point. Dickens sprang up from the hot water bottle with a gleam in his eye. "Well, hello, cat," I said. And I could see in an instant that I had correctly named him. He was going to be a rascally dickens all right. He crouched around corners waiting to spring at me as I passed by. He attacked my feet under the covers. He played until he dropped exhausted at my side.

Then it was time for my chemotherapy. Wendy went with me for the first round of treatment. I didn't learn until later how frightened she, too, had been.

I didn't realize what it was costing her emotionally to see her mother in this dire situation. Neither of us knew when (or if) I, like Dickens, might have *my* turning point.

I tolerated the first round of chemotherapy fairly well, and I thought I could make it through the remainder of the twenty-four treatments on my own. So I sent Wendy home to Seattle to take up her life with the understanding that if I couldn't get along without help, she would come back.

Twenty-one days after I began chemotherapy, my hair started coming out—great handfuls of it. I was ready with my wig and scarves. Just then Dickens decided my pillow was a good place to sleep. I don't know, perhaps he thought my balding head needed to be kept warm. I do know that in the mornings my pillow was a mess. It was covered with his fur and my hair, making it hard to tell who was shedding the most.

There were lots of nights during the next six months when I would wake from a deep sleep and be nauseated beyond belief. Dickens by now was sleeping in the crook of my arm. When I was sick, he'd jump to the end of the bed and wait. When I would lie down exhausted from vomiting, he would instantly jump back to my side and snuggle down. This little creature God had sent my way blessed my long, lonely nights.

Then there were the days Dickens raced me up the stairs. At my pace it wasn't much of a race, really. He romped and played and made me laugh and laugh and laugh. I tolerated the chemotherapy pretty well, and I am sure one reason was because Dickens gave me a merry heart that "did good, like medicine."

Then, at last I was through with chemo. All I had to do was wait. In October my surgeon said, "We'd like to do a second-look surgery. We can't find any cancer from the outside and we'd like to take a look inside."

This time my son, Mark, came to stay with me during surgery and to take care of Dickens. After only an hour in surgery, through my anesthesia-induced fog, I heard my very delighted surgeon say, "It's gone. There's no cancer anyplace."

I had my turning point! I was going to live. Five days later I went home, and while I couldn't scoop Dickens up (he now weighed fourteen pounds and I was not supposed to lift anything over ten), I sat down and he crawled into my lap. "Well, cat," I said, "it looks like I'm going to stick around for a while. We both made it. We're survivors." Dickens didn't say much. He just stretched a little and purred and purred.

Clover

Twila Bennett

I t was love at first sight.

For the cat anyway.

On a warm, August day, my family arrived at a cottage on a lake for a much needed break. Our lives had been stressful for the past few years. Several family members had passed away, jobs had grown chaotic, tempers were short; life had tumbled almost out of control. We had gone on other vacations during that time, but this one would be different. I was determined to relax. Interesting that we have to plan relaxation into our day, but for me in this week, it was going to happen.

Unpacking in the cottage, I looked out the window to see a flash of orange run by. My son yelled that a cat was on our porch, and he wondered aloud about her name.

Until my husband and I got a dog, I had never had a pet (I don't think hamsters count). So over the years, I've gotten used to and learned to love dogs. In fact, I adore them. But cats are another thing entirely. They are mysterious, temperamental, slinky, and they use their claws to inflict pain. Not my idea of a great pet.

So when my son found this cat, I was happy for him. An animal would entertain him while we were away from his friends. As I bent down to pet the cat, a woman rode by on a bike and yelled out that the cat was hers and that his name was Clover or Honey Clover as she liked to call him.

Him.

Hmmm.

As I looked at that cat, I wondered how in the world a fuzzy creature such as he could be a boy (I always assume cats are female).

Anyway, this guy was rubbing against me. Back and forth on my leg he went, meowing for all he was worth and purring like a little motor on the back of a boat. Pretty cute, that's for sure.

A little while later, I was drawn to the huge porch that encompassed the front of the cottage. There was a view of a park and the lake just beyond it. Huge trees hid the sky above and all I could hear were birds starting to settle in for the evening. Aah, paradise.

Immediately, there was a flash of orange.

Guess who?

Clover bounded to my chair. I decided to be nice and see if he would let me pet him. No need to ask twice, up he came. And so the dance began. That first evening, he was a flirt. Back and forth on the arms of the Adirondack chair, he whipped his tail and stared at me. Then he came in for a closer look. I reached up to pet him and he licked me. Cats lick? I never knew. I reached up again and he bit me. Not hard, just a little nip. I decided that I wouldn't pet him anymore.

So we sat content in and on the chair and watched the night, allowing ourselves simply to be happy in each other's company.

The next morning, I was drawn again to the porch. I brought out some hot tea and sat on the porch swing with my son. The day promised to be beautiful, and it was all the more special by a few moments shared with one of the loves of my life. And amazingly, the cat was back. He hopped up on the swing and immediately did a sashay around me, looking in my mug, sniffing my face, offering a sneaky lick, and off he went.

The little tease.

I began to realize that I was fascinated with this creature. Why would he pick me to be so interested in? He let my son pet him, but it seemed that he

the blue cat watches
yellow leaves spin to the earth
wishing they were birds

wanted me for a reason. I moved to the Adirondack chair and Clover jauntily leaped up on the arm. We worked out an agreement that he could lie on the arm while I petted him. No biting. No licking. My son moved off to parts unknown, and the cat and I sat and drank in the view.

Several evenings and mornings passed by, and we two became more attached. Clover leaped onto the porch at the sight of our car. He meowed at my window in the morning from the porch swing. He waited for me. He was persistent, that guy. Finally, one morning, he stretched out in my lap. This was new. He stayed for only a few minutes. He must have sensed my uneasiness (I was wearing shorts and those claws seemed to mean business!).

One night, my husband and son went fishing and left me to my porch and a brilliant sunset. I was prepared with jeans and a blanket when my friend visited. We immediately cuddled up in the chair as the night wind started to blow. The trees began to sway. The fishermen went inside, and I was left with the night noises and an incoming storm. The cat purred loudly. He vibrated my very insides while he lay on my chest, kneading me with his paws. He flopped on his side and I continued to pet him, albeit distractedly.

I can't explain it, but at that very moment I felt healing. Healing from loss, from worry, from stress. I wasn't attending to other people. I wasn't being pulled at from all sides. I wasn't being called or emailed or yelled at or ignored. I was being loved for being me and for the simple things I offered. Friendship, a warm lap, and undeniable devotion.

And it moved me to tears.

We feel so pulled in every direction. We feel beat up by people who say things that they probably don't mean, but they say them anyway. We are in positions at work that we love, but that we hate. Our families seem not to be able to live without our constant doing for them. Expectations are placed on us by others, but mostly by ourselves. The madness swirls around us and we can't seem to find what we are here to do or accomplish. And the pressure builds and builds and builds until we are not who we once were. We are not those simple children who had pie-in-the-sky dreams and desires.

In that minute, I realized that healing had begun. That orange flash had become my knight in shining armor. He had reminded me of the healing arms of a Father who offers true friendship, a warm lap, and undeniable devotion.

That cat didn't need something from me. I needed something from him.

The Way Back Home

Gregory L. Jantz, PhD

B renda's parents contacted us at The Center, desperate. They'd heard about our unique program for recovery from eating disorders. Brenda had already been in three hospital programs, including a critical care unit. One of these medical institutions put her in a straitjacket and tied her arms to the edge of the bed. Her parents said the hospital did this in order to force-feed their child.

At six years old, Brenda wouldn't eat. She was starving herself to death with anorexia. While other children her age were playing and exploring and taking joy in everyday life, Brenda was obsessed with starving. Anorexia was literally sucking the life out of her. When her parents brought her to us, she looked like one of those children in a commercial for third-world sponsorship.

Her parents said, "We need help. We're near bankruptcy. We've done all we know to do to help our daughter. And she just won't eat. Will you help us?"

I had a team meeting with our staff at The Center. After careful consideration, we decided that we would say yes to Brenda. We decided we would do all we could to make sure she lived. We wanted to have an opportunity to give her what we felt she hadn't received in the other programs or hospitals. We wanted to give her an opportunity not just to be treated but to be loved.

We decided beforehand that when little Brenda arrived we were going to get down on our hands and knees and play in our offices and do whatever she wanted to do. We weren't going to try to force her to conform to our world. We were going to do something totally different and trust that it would help. Brenda could not afford to have her weight go any lower. But nothing else had worked, so our therapeutic approach would be simply to love her.

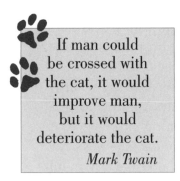

If man could be crossed with the cat, it would improve man, but it would deteriorate the cat.

Mark Twain

And so we did. We took turns sitting or lying on the floor, talking to Brenda, playing with her when she could play. Sometimes we wondered just how much she was able to understand, eating so infrequently. But we played with her, we talked with her, we listened to her, we loved her. We made as much eye contact as we possibly could, always trying to connect with her.

At first we could not tell if we were getting through. One day while I drove home, I began praying, "What else should we do for Brenda?" I drove by the local veterinarian's office. There in the window was a sign that read: "Free kittens." I found myself pulling into the parking lot.

Once inside, I was told at the desk there were only two kittens left, one of them the runt of the litter. Ed, the vet, brought out a cardboard box with an old towel on the bottom and two kittens curled up together in a corner. I could see that the littlest one was beyond being the runt. It was so small and sickly that it looked like it was going to die. I remember telling Ed, "You know, that's just the one I want. Thank you."

"No, this little thing is probably going to die," Ed cautioned. "You really don't want this kitten."

"No, no, I do want that one," I said. "I'll take it."

So Ed gave me the runt and a tube of sugared gel. We were supposed to see if the kitten would lick the sugar.

I took the kitten the next day to Brenda and said, "Sweetheart, your job is to keep this kitten alive." I put that pathetic little creature into her arms. She began to pet the kitten. She about wore the fur off that kitten, petting and petting her. From then on, wherever Brenda went, so went the kitten.

Just a few days later, little Brenda asked for food. The counselor who was with her at the time just about fainted. He came to me and asked, "What should I do?"

"Go back in and ask her what she wants," I said.

He did, and Brenda listed what she wanted to eat. We immediately went to the store and got everything she asked for. Then we sat in a circle, surrounding Brenda and the little runt of a kitten, and we all ate together. We all ate exactly what Brenda wanted to eat. It was difficult not to show how excited we were.

It might seem easier to make sense of this story if Brenda had been abused in some way as a child. That just wasn't the case. In fact, she came from a family that loved her greatly. We came to discover that someone, sometime, had made a rude and hurtful comment that Brenda overheard. It was the kind of comment adults offhandedly make in the presence of children, assuming they are too young to comprehend. But Brenda understood very well when this person made the comment that Brenda would always be fat. That comment struck at the very core of her being. Incredibly determined, even at six, Brenda decided she was not going to be fat. In fact, the more they forced her and put her in a straitjacket and stuck IVs in her arms and tubes down her nose, the more Brenda had refused to eat.

That was, until a little runt of a kitten.

I still get excited when I think of that moment. Little Brenda taught us something profound about release from the distortions of body and food and the lies of the world. She taught us that the way back home, and the way we create long-term change, is not through force but through love and acceptance.

While Brenda petted the little kitten over and over again, day after day, something wonderful was happening to the kitten, too. All of that touch was releasing growth hormones, and the kitten began to grow and thrive. Brenda's love for the kitten was likewise releasing in her a desire to live and to thrive. So she continued asking for food. When Brenda was given something to love that was safe, that kitten loved her back in ways we didn't fully realize at the time.

There came a time, of course, when Brenda and her parents were ready to return home and take up their lives, free of Brenda's eating disorder. After they returned home, the kitten found a home with my wife and me. She became part of our family and had several litters of her own kittens. We called them "therapy cats" and gave them away to bring love and healing to other families.

Small Miracles

Lonnie Hull DuPont

One chilly, rainy March evening, my husband, Joe, and I were getting ready to settle in for the night when we heard a small cry outside. Although we lived in a remote area, we were on a state road that had a fair number of big trucks. To hear such a small cry was unusual.

It got louder and more insistent. I looked out the front door, and there, sitting in a pool of light from our window, sat the homeliest little half kitten-half cat. She was all mouth, looking me right in the eye, crying for something to eat. She was around six months old, scrawny, and missing some teeth, and was she loud!

"What should we do?" my husband asked.

"We have to feed her out back," I said. "We can't let her go hungry." I thought for a moment and added, "And you have to do it. I'll get attached, and she's just going to get run over by a truck. You have to feed her."

My husband nodded. "I'm allergic to cats, so you know I won't get attached."

Famous last words. When Joe came in later, he was visibly moved. "She drooled right on the ground, she was so hungry," he reported. "But she rubbed and rubbed on me first, as if she were thanking me."

Joe fed her outside by the barn for the next several weeks. His allergies kept us from letting her in, but she seemed not to want to come inside anyway. She was skittish and seemed to like being outside as long as she was fed. She was clearly taking care of herself, not hounded by the wild animals around here. Spring came early and warm that year, so life wasn't too bad for the cat.

What Joe hadn't told me was that he and the cat were bonding. He would tap a can against the barn and she'd sashay her way to him, then rub on him. He'd pick her up, place her forehead against his, and they would just be that way for a while. Then he'd put her by her food where she hunkered down and ate. All the time she ate, Joe would pet her back really hard. She loved it. I think it made her feel safe, and in a primitive way, she had another creature literally to watch her back while she ate in the wild.

But we knew our place was dangerous. Strays never seemed to survive the truck traffic. And though it was spring, we knew winter in Michigan was no place for outdoor cats. We had no shelter for her—the barn was not ours and was locked up. We couldn't let her in the house because of Joe's allergy.

My brother-in-law offered to take her for his barn. He had a ranch and could use a mouser. That wouldn't be a bad life for a cat who seemed to like the outdoors. She'd have plenty of warm hay to sleep in and daily human interaction. So one night we put the cat in a travel box and drove the eight miles to the ranch. We talked soothingly to her, but she cried most of the way. At the ranch, she was unnerved, but eventually she sat down and ate, then began grooming. We left.

But I was in tears. I felt we'd abandoned an animal that had clearly been abandoned once before. Joe reminded me that we were trying to help a scrappy little cat survive, that it really was a good thing. I felt sick to my stomach about leaving her, but I had to agree.

Ten nights later, Joe walked by the front door and glanced out. There in a pool of light sat the cat, looking him straight in the eye, this time in silence.

"You won't believe this," Joe said. "Look."

Sure enough, there she sat, skinny and dirty. She had unusual markings so there was no doubt it was she. She had walked eight miles of swamps, cornfields, wild animals, dogs, and gun-happy people who hate cats, and she'd crossed the dangerous road of trucks to get to us.

Joe and I looked at each other. In unison we said, "She stays." We opened the door, and the little stray waltzed in as if she'd always lived here.

"What about your allergy?" I asked.

"I'll take a decongestant," Joe said. "This cat walked back to us."

Sure, You Could Buy Stock in Pet Stores

Visit your local farmers' market for cat "toys" that don't cost much. Rolling a grape tomato on a hard surface will turn most cats into a feline Pele. Feathers are also a hit, since cats are hardwired to deal with them. Farmers with peacocks may have feathers at molting time which they sell cheaply at farmers' markets. Ask for a deal on peacock feathers "without eyes"—tell them it's for your cat, and you may get freebies. But get a handful at a time; they're not indestructible by any means. Every time you pull out a fresh feather—or a new grape tomato—Mr. or Ms. Cat has a new toy.

Used to the outdoors, the cat had some trouble with that first night indoors. We did not know about the wisdom of confining a cat in a new environment. But she was exhausted, and after wolfing down food, she crawled under a cabinet and fell sound asleep. We named her Kit Kat after the kitchen clock.

The next day, Joe dropped Kit Kat off at a vet's for shots and spaying, and the following day we went to pick her up. There was bad news.

"Your cat has a terminal illness," the vet said. "When we opened her up, we saw that she has feline infectious peritonitis (FIP) in the advanced stage. Lots of strays and feral cats get this. She is asymptomatic right now, but she isn't going to live a long life."

We were devastated. After much questioning, it turned out that Kit Kat probably didn't even have a year. "We can put her down now if you'd like," the vet offered.

Before I had a chance to respond, Joe said firmly, "Absolutely not. This cat worked hard to get to us. We'll take her home and keep her until she dies."

And so we took home our terminal cat. That night, with stitches in her belly, a devastating diagnosis, and a fresh pedicure, she caught a mouse. Its corpse lay neatly next to Kit Kat when we woke up. We were very pleased.

Something else was going on in my life at the time. I was adopted at birth and had found the whereabouts of my biological mother many years ago. I wrote to her several times—even asked for medical history—but she never answered my letters. I had never met her.

But I was soon to learn that the very night we took Kit Kat to the ranch, my biological mother died in a nearby town. Three days later, her friends tracked me down. They hadn't known she had a child at all until shortly before she died, and then only because they came across my letters. The letters were kept together in a place near her reading chair. She could never bring herself to respond to me.

The day after we brought Kit Kat home from the vet, I went to my birth mother's memorial service. I learned that she had a wonderful laugh and that her confirmation verse had been "Make a joyful noise unto the Lord." I learned that her favorite song was "Mack the Knife," a detail I found particularly delightful for some reason. And that, like me, she was a voracious reader. I got to know her friends and my relatives. I was so happy that I had at least this much. Probably only adopted people can really understand this, but at the age of forty-six, for the first time in my life I felt grounded.

But I couldn't grieve. I felt distanced. After all, I did not know this woman. She gave birth to me, but I never knew her. I felt oddly detached among the mourners. I only wished she would have consented to see me before dying.

Back home, however, I suddenly found all kinds of maternal feelings rising in me toward Kit Kat. I have no children and had never felt these feelings before. But I found myself rocking Kit Kat and crying. Why was I crying? On the surface, I didn't want my little cat to die. But I also knew that she was the vehicle to help me connect to my deeply buried grief about the woman who bore me but would not know me.

Kit Kat would tolerate my attention for a while, then she would jump down and go about her cat day. And I'd feel better. But I always prayed that I'd be able to handle it when she got sick.

Months went by. Kit Kat didn't get sick. She got big and sleek and turned into a gorgeous tortoiseshell. She was smart and quick, and she lived for Joe, who would get down on the floor and play with her. She still liked us to watch her while she ate. Sometimes if we left her alone for the day, she wouldn't eat until we came back and sat with her at her cat dish.

Joe took drugs for his allergies, and we agreed to keep Kit Kat out of the bedroom, thereby keeping one room dander-free. But Joe's allergy simply disappeared. Now both my cat and my husband were healthier than they were expected to be.

After a few months, I took Kit Kat in for a claw trim. It was the same clinic but a different vet. "How do you think her FIP is?" I asked.

The vet looked at me, then back at Kit Kat. "This cat has FIP?" she asked. "Who told you that?"

I paused. "This clinic told me."

The vet looked a little uncomfortable. "Did they see it in wet stages when they operated on her?"

"Yes," I said. "Doesn't she have it?"

"Well," she drawled, "sometimes other things look like FIP. The fact that your cat not only did not get sick but got healthier makes me wonder. I'm not saying she has it, but I'm not saying she doesn't, either."

So I took Kit Kat home, hardly daring to believe she might not die so soon.

Right around that time, I had a dream. It had been six months since my biological mother died, and in the dream, I was told that I could visit her. I went up in a jet. She entered it mid-flight from the back of the plane and came down the aisle, beaming at me. She sat next to me and curled around me, never speaking, just smiling. I told her all about myself, about my childhood, and about my love of books. She nodded and almost cooed, but she never spoke.

I felt love radiate from her, and I felt something strongly maternal flow from her. I almost expected her to count my fingers and toes. I had the realization that in the next life, we get to be the individual God created each of us to be, before our walls go up and cloak parts of our individual selves.

Eventually I knew she had to leave. She held my hand, still silent. Then she got up, walked back down the aisle, and disappeared.

When I woke up, I felt almost as though I had had a visitation. I felt that in a way, I knew my birth mother now, and I felt so very sorry that she could not bring down her own walls enough to know me in this life. For the first time, I felt grief. I cried for days.

Kit Kat now began climbing on me and kneading her paws into me as if she were nursing. She treated me like I was her mother. I felt terribly protective. I felt her little claws and loved her and cried. I didn't think I could stand to lose her.

I took her to a different vet.

"This cat does not have FIP," the vet proclaimed. "If she did, she'd be dead by now, and she certainly wouldn't be this hale and hearty."

cats run over us
pulling sheets onto the floor
the moon disappears

I consulted a third vet who said the same.

"Do you mean I might have her for many years?" I asked this one.

"No reason why not."

At this writing, Kit Kat is a husky, frisky nine-year-old cat who is madly in love with Joe. My maternalism toward her relaxed, and my grief about my birth mother turned into the dull ache it needs to be. Kit Kat has a cat-sister now—another stray who showed up crying at the door. Joe and I often remark that we don't know what we did without these two cats.

So did Kit Kat ever have FIP? Probably not, though I have friends who believe love healed her. Whatever the case may be, we're thankful every day that she survived and walked back to us.

We live in a fallen world. Kittens are thrown into the wild by cruel people. Mothers can't always keep their babies. But there are also small miracles: Kit Kat finding us, my people finding me, Kit Kat insisting that she is ours, Joe losing his allergy, my meeting my mother in a vivid dream, Kit Kat's clean bill of health. These are the things for which I am grateful. These are ways I know my Creator watches over me.

A Mocha's Just What I Needed

Amy J. Tol

I'm a dog person. Or so I thought, as I sipped my hot chocolate and studied a variety of doggie handbooks. Unfortunately, I hadn't yet found a canine variety that fit my simple requirements. All I wanted was a big dog who wouldn't mind living in a tiny house. A dog with a bladder that could handle all-day absences while my husband and I worked and a calm personality that wouldn't go haywire every time the doorbell rang. And I was hoping for something inexpensive. And easy to train.

And was it asking too much to expect that he'd clean up his own messes in the yard?

It wasn't the first time I'd looked through dog books, and it wasn't the first time my husband shook his head at me and gently reminded me that "we aren't really at a good stage of life for having a dog right now, honey."

My brain agreed completely. But that didn't stop my heart from longing for a furry friend.

And apparently it didn't stop my husband from thinking about it either. Because one day, while I was sipping a cup of joe at work, the phone rang. It was Brian—my groom of just over a year—and he had an interesting proposition for me.

"I know we've been talking about getting a dog lately . . ." he started. *Calling about a dog while he's at work?*

I mused. *He wouldn't call unless he was serious about this. Has he just heard about some new and exotic breed that will be our perfect fit? One of those creative mixes like a Cockapoo-poo or something?* Ready to hear about our perfect canine concoction, I almost spit out my coffee at his next words.

"Well, how would you feel about a cat?"

A cat? Are you crazy? I hate cats. Don't you remember that horrible house-sitting experience I had in college? The one with the four cats who jumped all over me by day, scratched unceasingly at the bedroom door by night, and even had the nerve to claw and bruise my arm simply because I was restraining them from getting out of the house? Horrible, annoying creatures.

Fortunately, I was in too much shock to actually put a voice to any of these thoughts. So my husband continued, "My co-worker found this litter of kittens in her backyard a few days ago and the mother hasn't come back. She's going to take them to the humane society unless anyone at work wants them. Do you think we should take one?"

Now as I said, I wasn't a big fan of cats. In fact I'd vowed—with great passion and zeal—never to own one. But the prospect of some poor abandoned creature being put to sleep at the humane society? Well, my heart's not made of stone.

"I don't know," I finally managed to get out. "A cat? We've never talked about a cat before. . . ." And because I had to convince myself we were really having this discussion, I added, "We're talking about a cat here, right?"

My husband sensed that my muddled mind couldn't respond with a coherent thought. So he suggested that I think about it and call him back when I made my decision. But I panicked at the prospect of having to determine some pitiful kitten's fate.

"Why don't you just decide, Brian. I'll be fine either way." I must have sounded convincing because he agreed to this proposal. And I spent the rest of the workday vacillating between hope that a kitten might make a tolerable pet and horror that I was considering such a prospect.

When my husband picked me up from work that evening, it took one glance in the backseat to discover that our family had just grown: a tiny calico looked up at me, let out a most pitiful meow, and then allowed me to stroke the fur on her quaking back. Surprised by the incredible softness of her coat, I picked her up and held her against my chest for a moment.

And what can I say? She started to purr. And that's when I started to become a cat person.

We brought the fluffy creature home and after some deliberation settled on the name Mocha—perfect for a white kitten accented with coffee- and chocolate-colored spots. She settled in quickly, spending most of the day sleeping in a basket I'd lined with soft towels.

This kitten might have gotten under my skin a little, but she wasn't about to gain the run of the house. I had standards after all. No cat—no matter how cute—was about to destroy the stylish atmosphere I'd created in our cozy bungalow.

So of course, she wouldn't be allowed to jump on any furniture she pleased. And she'd have to sleep outside the bedroom because the door would be closed to her. And she most certainly would have to stay away from my garden window full of artfully displayed houseplants.

Mocha missed the memo on every point. She sidelined the furniture rule by catching me at my weakest point: Who can resist a purring kitten cozying up next to them during a weekend nap on the couch? And we hadn't anticipated that she'd be tiny enough to crawl under the bedroom door at night, so she soon jumped and wiggled her way to the foot of the bed as well. By the time she started sunning herself among my plants in the garden window, I'd given up on having any control whatsoever.

By the two-month mark, it was official: Mocha became queen of the house.

Since I'd given up any hope of controlling where Mocha might roam, it was no surprise that she nosed her way into trouble. There was the time she batted so many toys into a basement drain that it became completely stopped up. And the moment when she set her tail on fire—oblivious to the fact she'd been holding it over a scented candle.

But I think her most memorable foible may have actually been a ploy to harmonize the home. It was a weekday evening and my husband and I were discussing finances when the eternal question of the ages sparked debate: Should we buy whole life or term insurance? What started as a simple argument soon turned into a battle of the wills, each of us determined to convince the other of the error of his or her way. The newlywed glow had turned into a glower.

> The fact is that, to cats, we humans are, for all our grotesque size, unbelievably slow and clumsy. We are totally incapable of managing a good leap or jump or pounce or swipe or, indeed, almost any other simple maneuver which, at the very least, would make us passable fun to play with.
>
> *Cleveland Amory*

Enter the cat. Bedraggled. Waterlogged. And smelling like laundry detergent.

The best we can figure it, the cat had jumped onto the washing machine to watch water draining to a nearby washtub. She had often perched on the sink's edge, poking her little paw into the stream of rinse water. So it wasn't hard to imagine that she might have lost her balance and ended up taking an unexpected dip in the suds. Fortunately, she made her way out of the water and dripped her way up the stairs. As wet as she was, she probably figured she could dry off in the heat of our argument.

Which might have worked if our anger hadn't dissolved into laughter at the sight of her Royal Dripping

Highness. She was a mess, with fur sticking up, suds on her nose, and two tired eyes seeming to ask how she could have fallen to such an undignified state.

I scooped her up while Brian fetched the towels. And by the time we'd finished blow-drying her fur and settling her onto a bed of blankets atop the couch, our argument had been forgotten. Harmony was restored. And the queen was still on her throne.

The thing about living with royalty is that you never become too consumed with yourself. They are always there to remind you that there's a higher power in control.

I guess that's what Mocha was thinking on the day I started rehearsing music on the piano. I'd selected a song for that week's church service, and I started to sing through the vocals while my fingers danced along the keys. Just when I was starting to mentally admire the product of my musical prowess, I suddenly found a set of paws in the middle of the keyboard and a pink tongue licking my nose.

I'm not sure if Mocha was enjoying the music or simply trying to make it stop. But every time I started to sing for the next several months, I'd suddenly find a cat in my lap and a tongue on my face. I'd pluck her up and set her gently back to the ground. But as soon as my voice broke into song, she'd be right back in my lap, giving a generous gift of kitty saliva to my nose.

After a while, I stopped trying to set her down. I'd just flip her around in my lap and let her sit there while I continued to play. It was an arrangement that seemed to suit us both.

And in the end, that's the arrangement this doggie fanatic has embraced. I still think cats can be annoying. They sometimes act horribly rude. And they certainly have attitude issues. But they also snuggle up to you on a cold winter night, purr away your stress, and lick your tear-stained face on the days that get you down.

So I'm joining the club. I'm pinning on the badge. And I'll admit the truth: I'm a cat lover now. And all because God dismissed my doggie dreams and set me on an unexpected feline adventure. He must have known that on my journey of busy days, heavy issues, and constant stress, I'd need a Mocha along for the ride.

Mittens
Marci Alborghetti

O n my ninth birthday, my parents gave me a
kitten. He was gorgeous, with blue gray fur
and white paws. Being extraordinarily creative even at that tender age, I named him Mittens.

There was no question about who Mittens belonged
to. Not only was he the most precious birthday present
I'd ever received, he seemed to know he was mine.
Even as a kitten, he would follow me around the yard
and house. He was affectionate with my younger sister
and parents, but I was the one he came to at the first
call. Of course, it might have had something to do
with the fact that I was also the one who fed him!

During our first months together, we spent most of
our time outdoors exulting in the brief Connecticut
summer. My birthday was in July, so we had several
weeks of freedom before school started. I used this
time wisely, constructing our home out of a series

of lawn chairs, old sheets, and cardboard. After this elegant residence was completed, I cushioned a sturdy box with old towels and sheets, fashioned a little bonnet, tied it around Mittens' neck, and laid him lovingly in his bassinet. My "baby" and I passed many an afternoon protected from the sun in our little home, only occasionally inviting my sister and neighborhood kids to join our domestic tranquility.

Looking back now, I can't believe my patient kitten tolerated such behavior. Most cats would have darted away and adopted another owner at the very sight of my clever tent/house. Not Mittens. He seemed to recognize my childish solitude and instinctively understand my loneliness. Cats may have a reputation as solitary, aloof creatures, but Mittens kept me company regardless of my overactive imagination and annoying housekeeping schemes.

But it wasn't until months later that I realized just how close our bond had grown.

In April Mittens went missing. I called him one night before bed, and he didn't return. This was so uncharacteristic, I knew immediately that something was wrong. We lived on a relatively busy road, and my first horrified thought was that he'd been hit by a car.

light rain comes inside
tortoiseshell at the window
licks her body dry

Imagining him struggling, hurt and bleeding in some gulch, sent me running in tears to my father. To his everlasting credit he put me in the car, and we cruised slowly up and down the road looking for Mittens or signs of an accident. We found neither, and I spent a long night tossing and turning in my little bed. Mittens had become an indispensable member of our family by then, and I don't think any of us slept that night. Even my mother, who pretended to complain when Mittens pranced daintily through her immaculate, well-organized kitchen cabinets, had red-rimmed, dark-circled eyes the next morning when she made us breakfast.

I fussed anxiously about going to school and jumped on my bike as soon as I returned. I rode endlessly up and down the streets of our neighborhood, alertly looking for my cat. I asked everyone I saw about Mittens, but no one had a clue.

By the third afternoon I knew in my heart, as a child does, that my parents had given up. But I couldn't. I flew up and down our street on my bike, calling out for Mittens, my eyes everywhere at once.

Suddenly, a brief movement caught my eye. I stopped short, studying the line of windows on our elderly neighbor's garage door. Mrs. Smithhurst had closed down her house in the fall to make her annual pilgrimage south for the winter. The house, garage, and yard were completely still as they had been for months now. After several minutes, I sighed and prepared to ride away.

There it was again! A flashing movement barely visible through the clouded garage door windows! I dropped my bike in the road and sped up the deserted driveway. Standing on my tiptoes, I could just reach the dirty windows which I frantically wiped with my hand. I peered through the small, smudged circle I'd hastily created. There was Mittens, thin and bedraggled, but staring up hopefully as though he'd been expecting me!

I was immediately seized with a dilemma so wrenching it turned my joy to tears. I knew I couldn't free him—everything was locked!—but the last thing I wanted to do was leave him again to fetch my father. Struggling with an anguish I can still feel over thirty years later, I shouted assurances of my swift return to him and fled down the street for my father.

It was just a few minutes later when we returned, but it seemed like eons to me as I imagined my poor kitten watching in despair as my familiar face at the window had vanished. In that short time, my mind painted an agonizing picture of how Mittens had been trapped listening to my futile calls for three solid days and nights. He'd most likely been leaping up and down in the air for the entire time, just hoping I'd spot him. Yet I'd been cycling by again and again, hardly giving Mrs. Smithhurst's boarded up house a second glance. And now that I'd found him and then immediately disappeared, he must be lying there thinking I'd abandoned him again.

Night Time May or May Not Be the Right Time

While it's true that cats see well in the dark, they are not truly nocturnal creatures. Sure, they'll hunt at night. But not all night. Cats are high on the food chain and are able to sleep away two-thirds of their life—sixteen hours a day for the average domestic cat. Most likely, while we're sleeping, our cats are sleeping too— sometimes very comfortably on top of our feet.

Cats are neither nocturnal nor diurnal creatures; they are crepuscular, meaning they come to life at dawn and dusk. That's when their traditional food source is on the move. Why does this matter to you and your house cat? Because Mr. Cat is especially alert at dawn and dusk and would like to play at those times. Remember, all cat play is really about hunting live food, which means that when you dangle a string, Mr. Cat sees a tail. So when you have your morning coffee and when you come home from work, dangle a toy for your feline for some quality cat time. Then maybe the little beast will stop attacking your feet while you sleep.[2]

Yet when we returned and looked in the garage window, Mittens was sitting in the same spot, his eyes fixed unwaveringly on the circle in the window where he'd first seen my face.

My father, in his own way no less distressed than I, wasted no time removing a windowpane. Fortunately,

Mrs. Smithhurst was an immaculate lady; you could virtually eat off her garage floor. Though there'd been nothing for Mittens to eat, he had managed to drink from several puddles of relatively clean water that had seeped into the garage after the spring rains. He was weak and scrawny when I scooped him up, but the vet said he'd be fine.

Many times in my life since then I've felt trapped and afraid. Many times I've felt abandoned and alone. Many times I've faced an unknown outcome that seemed impossibly bleak. But I try to remember Mittens with his unwavering, trustful gaze and certain faith. And at those moments I think to myself, "Wait for the Lord. Take courage, and wait for the Lord."

The Cat Who Rescued the Boy

Linda S. Clare

I stood on the back deck and shivered in the crisp October morning. It had been below freezing for two nights—unusual for an Oregon autumn, but it matched my mood. "Why, God?" I prayed. "Why can't my son behave?"

A day earlier my sixteen-year-old, Nate, had been caught smoking near the high school. He and a friend had climbed into a tree to hide their activity. Now he was suspended from school for a week. I was so hurt and angry I almost wanted him to disappear.

His ten-year-old sister, Alyssa, interrupted my prayer. "Mom," she said frantically, "I can't find Oliver. He's gone!" A few weeks before, she'd rescued the orange and white shorthair kitten from a home where the owners did little more than throw dry cat chow onto their patio. We'd spent his first day combing his short fur free of fleas and plant burrs. But even before Ollie was old enough to roam, he liked to misbehave. *Just like my son*, I thought. Alyssa's insistence jerked me back to the missing kitten.

"We have to find him, Mom!" Her eyebrows bunched with worry. "I can't go to school until I know my Oliver's home safe!" She burst into tears.

"What's up?" My son walked out onto the deck where we stood. Alyssa wiped her tears with her arm.

"Ollie's gone!" Alyssa wailed. "Get Ollie back, okay, Nate?"

In typical teen fashion, Nate shrugged. "How should I know where he went?" he said, and I shot him an angry look. He avoided my gaze and added, "Hey, I'll try."

Try! If he tried a little harder at school instead of getting into trouble, I'd be a lot happier. It was time for school so I reassured Alyssa and sent her off, promising to scour the neighborhood. Nate had to clean out the garage, partial penance for disappointing his family. He slunk away to do his chore. I swept leaves from the deck, scanning the horizon, hoping for some answers to my prayers.

Then I saw it: a glint of red near the top of our neighbor's towering fir. Ollie had a bright red collar. But that tree was enormous—how could a kitten climb so high?

"Oliver," I yelled. Cold air stung my eyes as I searched the dark boughs. A "meow" floated down. Somehow Ollie got stuck in the tallest tree around on the coldest morning of the year. He was at least seventy-five feet up. I ran inside and called the fire department.

I was shocked when the dispatcher said, "Sorry, we don't rescue kittens from trees. That's on TV. Try the utility company."

I ran back outside to comfort Ollie. He meowed every time I shouted his name, but now other voices joined in. Several large crows—or were they ravens?— circled around, their caws loud and coarse. They dived at Oliver again and again. I hurried back inside to phone the utility company.

"You're outside the city limits, ma'am," the woman said. "We don't service your area. And anyway our ladders only extend fifty feet."

"I know he's up higher than fifty feet." I tried not to cry. "Doesn't anybody care about a poor kitten?" The crows were making a racket. I imagined Ollie clinging to the branch in terror.

The sun had warmed the day but by noon things were no better. I'd been standing out there all morning, alternately praying and coaxing the frightened kitten to climb down. To make matters worse, the tree was in our neighbor's backyard and the man was away at work. He also owned two huge dogs fierce enough to warrant a "Beware of Dog" sign on his fence. The night before, the temperature had dropped to seventeen degrees—I doubted any kitten could survive another freezing night without food or water. But I wasn't giving up.

Three hours later my voice was reduced to a hoarse whisper. I'd screamed at the crows and kept up a pep talk for Ollie, whose own cries were getting fainter by the minute. I told him to "hang in there," and visualized that poster of a kitten hanging from a bar by its paws. But I also knew he was in serious trouble.

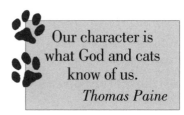

Our character is what God and cats know of us.

Thomas Paine

The crows must have had a nest near where he clung, because they didn't let up. Their black shiny wings shone as they struck and Ollie yowled in pain each time. How much more could the poor thing take? "Please, God," I whispered, "please let help come soon." As if he had heard my prayer, Ollie let out a weak cry.

When our neighbor finally got home, school was nearly over. Alyssa would be here any minute. I called to Nate, still toiling away in the garage, and we raced next door. The man secured his dogs and brought out his tallest ladder, but the top step was several feet below the bottom branch of the tree.

I knew from the incident at school that my son was an expert climber. But I couldn't dwell on his mistakes now. "Don't worry, Mom," Nate said. He clambered up the ladder. "I'll save Ollie." He grabbed the bottom branch and hoisted his body up. I smiled at him.

Nate scaled the huge tree toting a Strawberry Shortcake pillowcase—to keep Ollie from scratching or jumping—just as Alyssa burst into the yard. We prayed for Nate to be sure-footed, and Alyssa screamed at the crows to leave her kitty alone. Finally her big brother descended, a squirming lump in the pillow-case. We rushed back to our house and inspected Ollie's injuries.

The kitten had several deep cuts where the crows had assailed him, but he gobbled a bowl of food topped off with a drink of water. Then he crawled into Alyssa's lap and closed his eyes. Before long, Alyssa fell asleep as well.

But Nate and I were working in the kitchen. He leaned against the counter and peeled the potatoes I'd set out for him. He wouldn't look at me.

"Son," I said, "you know what you did was . . ."

He turned to face me. "I know, I know, it was wrong. I'm sorry." He looked up, his eyes glistening with tears. "I'll never do it again."

I placed my hand gently on his shoulder. "I was going to say that what you did was *heroic*—rescuing Ollie that is. But you're paying the consequences. I love you and I'm proud of what you did to save the kitten."

"Really?"

"Just don't go climbing trees for the wrong reason, okay?" We laughed. Oliver padded into the kitchen and rubbed against his rescuer's leg, as if to say, "Thanks."

I'd been so angry that I wanted my son to disappear, but God knew better. That day, God took trouble and brought redemption to a tiny cat and a repentant boy.

Heroes, I thought, *aren't hard to find. You just have to be willing to go out on a limb.*

Angel

Lisa-Anne Wooldridge

T hat one, Mom!" I pleaded, pointing at the only female kitten in the litter. "I'm gonna name her Angel!" My brother and sister each chose a kitten, too, and for the rest of the day we did nothing but carry them around.

It was a hard season in my young life. I didn't fit in well in my small town school, friends were few and far between, and my parents were dealing with emotional and financial hardships. I desperately needed something to love that would love me back.

Angel was a tuxedo kitty, colored black and white; her mannerisms were dainty and perfectly ladylike. She seemed to listen when I talked and would sometimes respond with little purring meows.

As she grew, she decided to follow me everywhere. She'd trek with me for miles into the woods. She would spend hours sunning herself while I picked blackberries for pies and cobblers. Her faithfulness and constancy were just the comfort that I needed.

She slept next to me, at least until I fell asleep. I struggled with nightmares, and many nights it would be Angel who would wake me from them, patting my face with her paws. Even when she'd been left out for the night, she'd come to my window and meow and paw the glass until I woke up. She never did it on the nights when I had good dreams!

She had some amazing talents. One day I watched her organize her two brother cats into a team. She jumped up and grabbed our front door knob with her paws and twisted while the two males each pushed on the door with their heads. The door opened, and the satisfied trio let themselves in. That explained why we kids were always getting in trouble for leaving the door open.

Every school day she'd walk me to the top of our hill, and then I'd send her home. After school, she never failed to be waiting for me on the sidewalk about a block from home. She would be there at exactly 2:35. How she was able to tell time so perfectly I'll never know.

It seemed to me that Angel was never afraid. She'd climb trees to sit in my lap; she'd even follow me out on a branch over a pond I called my "reflecting pool." She always seemed to know when I needed her and would seek me out when I was afraid or lonely or crying. Once she ran ahead of me and flushed out a copperhead snake hiding where I liked to play. Her quick thinking drove the snake away and protected me from being bitten.

Angel stayed with me for four of the hardest years of my life. Very often she was the tangible expression of God's comfort and love to me. I believe he sent her to help me over the rough spots, to give me joy and peace, to remind me of his constant, watchful care. I'd named her Angel impulsively, as a child. As a grown woman, I don't have any doubts. She was absolutely one of God's messengers to me. She touched my heart with the wonder of his love.

60

The Peacemaker

Callie Smith Grant

It was early evening, late November, when I pulled into the driveway of our remote farmhouse. I gathered my things and opened the car door. An audible wind came from the southwest and blustered around the corner of the house. With it came a sound I didn't want to hear—the cry of a small animal.

A stray cat? I hoped not. It was thirteen degrees out there, and snow was predicted.

I braced against the wind and rounded the corner of the house. As soon as the utility light at the back door flashed on, out of the blackness sprang the most gorgeous kitten I had ever seen. She was a solid smoky gray and so beautiful and so panicked that I'm embarrassed to say I actually burst into tears.

The kitten beat me to the door and expressed tremendous relief at seeing me. Of course, intense rubbing and purring kicked in, the ways of a cat in need. This kitten apparently had been around people enough to know to come to them for protection, and she was using everything in her power to get help. I put down my bags and bent down to pet her.

I felt a little sick to my stomach because I knew I could not bring her inside. My husband and I had a territorial tortoiseshell house cat who was not sociable to other animals. We feared she'd do harm to another feline, especially a small one. I also knew better than to expose strange cats to one another since so many feline diseases run rampant in the outdoors.

I unlocked the door to the house, and I had quite a time keeping her from going in. I told her I'd be right back, but of course she didn't understand. I gently nudged her back with my toe and managed to get myself indoors where I opened a can of cat food and filled a dish of water.

When I opened the door again, I saw that the kitten had managed to tuck herself in between the storm door and the back door, and there she huddled on the threshold, trying to get warm. This broke my heart. I gently nudged her off the threshold and stepped back outside with her, talking in soothing tones. When I placed the dishes on the deck, she hunkered down to eat with gusto. Then I sneaked back indoors and watched her from the window.

The problem was that my husband, Mike, and I already had our house cat, BatGirl. We loved BatGirl very much, but she was an acquired taste—a husky, tough exterior housing a truly soulful creature. And

C. S. Lewis and His "Stepcat"

After the death of his beloved wife, Joy, C. S. Lewis found unexpected comfort in her cats. He wrote: "Joy's Siamese—my 'stepcat' as I call her—is the most terribly conversational animal I ever knew. She talks all the time and wants doors and windows to be opened for her 1,000 times an hour. . . . She adores me because I lift her up by her tail—an operation which I can't imagine I should like if I were a cat, but she comes back for more and more, purring all the time. . . . How strange that God brings us into such intimate relations with creatures of whose real purpose and destiny we remain forever ignorant."[3]

BatGirl, also a stray, had fended for herself outside too long to get along with competition. She was an absolute sweetheart unless confronted by another creature. She backed my mother's dog right into a corner. So we never considered bringing in another cat—we figured our cat would kill a newcomer. So we had decided ours would be a one-pet house. It was a while before we would learn that house cats killing one another would be highly unlikely.

Through the window, I saw Mike pull in the driveway from work. I continued to watch the little gray kitten work her way through the can of cat food as Mike walked indoors and looked at me. "So what's the story out there?"

I didn't know what was wrong with me, but I started crying again. "She's a stray," I blubbered. "We can't leave her out there or she'll freeze to death. And we can't have her inside because BatGirl will kill her."

Mike nodded and thought for a minute. "Listen, we never put anything back in that upstairs bedroom after we painted it." It was true. Our old house was cavernous, and we didn't use the upstairs, which was shut off from the main floor. "We have another litter box," Mike continued. "Let's put the kitten in the empty room until we can figure out what to do with her. At least she'll be warm and safe, and BatGirl won't be able to get to her."

It was a good plan. "Okay," I sniffed. I put Bat-Girl in the basement as Mike headed out the back door. When he brought in the kitten, her purr was so noisy it preceded her like an announcement. I've since learned that kittens have loud purrs so that Momma can hear them. Well, this human momma definitely heard her.

"Careful," Mike said, "her nose is bleeding. She may be diseased."

We wrapped her in my pink bath towel, and I held her on her back like a baby. The little thing purred and wiggled, and tears sprang up in my eyes again. I felt like an idiot crying over this kitten, but there it was.

"I don't know if she's bleeding from her nose or if it's a scrape," Mike observed, looking her over. Now that we had some light, we could see that she was a female, around five months old, short-haired but with a soft, thick coat. She was a solid gray—the shade of gray called blue in a cat—from her triangular head to her tapered paws, even her straight nose and velvety ears. She gazed back and forth at us, sea-green eyes peering out of that smoky coat like headlights in fog.

"Wow," said Mike. "This cat could be in a calendar." Indeed, she was perfectly and beautifully made. We oohed and aahed over her, and I started to calm down once I realized her sweet nature and exceptional beauty would guarantee her a home. Certainly someone would take her. In fact, since any stray out there was a drop-off, it was hard to imagine anyone giving up this lovely creature with what seemed to be a winning personality.

Eventually Mike took her from me. "I'll get her bedded down," he offered. "She's probably exhausted."

Never was there a happier feline than the blue kitten that night. We made her a bed in a box with an old sweater of mine to keep her warm, and Mike took her upstairs. We realized later that between the towel and the sweater, she learned to take comfort from my scent right away. Mike fixed a litter box for her, and she leaped right in, tossed sand around a bit, and had a private moment. She devoured another bowl of food, purring the entire time, then curled up in her new bed and watched Mike putter around her new room from under heavy eyelids. Her relief was palpable.

I stayed downstairs on the phone, trying to find her a home, but to no avail. We were going to have to house her for a while. Mike agreed to take care of her since I had such an emotional reaction to a kitten we were going to give away.

The next morning, when Mike went upstairs to feed the kitten, she had cleaned herself up. Now it was clear that her nose was only scraped. In a few days, we took her to our vet for a checkup and vaccinations. She purred through the entire appointment—even the shots. She certainly was a sweet kitten.

She stayed upstairs in her room for the next several days. At first she kept rather quiet up there, and we figured she was getting rested up from her harrowing time outdoors. We didn't think she'd been outside long, but certainly she'd expended plenty of energy during that time trying to survive.

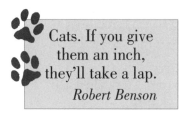

Cats. If you give them an inch, they'll take a lap.
Robert Benson

After a week had gone by, one night Mike put BatGirl in the basement and brought the kitten downstairs, thinking I might want to hold her. He was right. I placed her on her back and cradled her. She let me rub her downy belly and even gently separate and rub each of her toes. She always kept her claws in. At one point she stretched out her front paw and placed it on my cheek, keeping it there while she gazed into my face.

Oh dear. How was I going to give her away?

For the next few weeks, The Little One, as we began calling her, lived in her room. When Mike poured new litter into her box, she sat on his shoulder to watch. When he poured dry food into her dish, she dove under the bag and let the food pellets rain on her. When he rolled the trash can to the roadside in the moonlight or raked leaves in the front yard in daylight, she watched from a tall upstairs window. She pounced on any toy we gave her, especially rubber balls—she played and played with them in her otherwise empty room.

As for me, I would lie in bed in the room below and listen to the small cat roll the ball back and forth on the pine floor planks early in the morning and late at night, then scamper after it. Though I refused to name a cat I was planning to give away, in my heart I came up with the name Lucy because of the ball—Lucille Ball.

Of course we knew we couldn't keep The Little One. Besides the matter of BatGirl and her territoriality, Mike and I both drove long distances for our work—or for anything at all—and we were seldom home to deal with a kitten, especially one as curious and rambunctious as this one was turning out to be. BatGirl had been extremely low-maintenance as a youngster, and we were not prepared for the liveliness of this kitten.

So we continued to work at finding a home for The Little One. Over the next few weeks, three different families each gave a definite yes. Then at the last minute, for a variety of reasons, none could take her. This was frustrating, because I knew that if anyone would hold her just once, they'd walk away with her. I knew this because I'd fallen in love with her myself.

I gave in and began going upstairs every day, several times per day, to give the kitten some attention. She was getting pretty lonely and bored up there by herself. So every day I would place her on her back and hold her in my arms like a baby. I'd learned from some cat rescuers that it's good to get kittens adjusted to being touched on their bellies, and The Little One grew to like it. She would literally gaze up at me and heave a sigh, the picture of contentment and peace while I held her. Sometimes she'd reach her paw up to my face, sometimes both her paws, to press against my chin, purring and looking into my eyes.

To say I was smitten would be an understatement. I adored this little cat. She also had a calming effect on me. I'm prone to anxiety, and I found myself relaxing whenever I held her. At such times I focused only on her. But I refused to speak her name out loud, and I redoubled my efforts to find her a good home before it became too hard to let her go.

I am a praying person. I pray about many things, but with so much misery in the world, should I beseech God on behalf of one blue kitten in winter? I decided, yes, the creatures of the world are here for reasons beyond my understanding. So as I held and played with The Little One, I did pray for her future.

After so many close calls for a home for her, I started to feel a little panicky. I began to ask in my prayers, "Who else can I call?" And one day after she'd been with us just over a month, I distinctly heard inside me, *She's yours.*

I protested right back inside. "I can't have her."

Again I heard, *She's yours.*

It was a voice that had never failed me before. I quieted down inside and let the idea settle in. I held The Little One a bit more, then I put her in her box-bed and went downstairs.

I called my husband, and without my bringing up any of this, he said to me, "You know, some people here at the office are sure we can get the cats together if we take our time with them. Apparently there are ways to do it. So I was thinking, since we'll both be home the week between Christmas and New Year, let's keep The Little One and use that time to get her together with BatGirl."

Besides feeling stunned that Mike and I would be so in sync about this, I realized that it made perfect sense. Maybe it could work. Maybe The Little One really was ours.

I went back upstairs, picked the kitten up, and for the first time whispered into her satiny ear, "Lucy. . . ."

She purred and purred.

That night Mike and I called a pet behaviorist we knew to help us. We didn't want things to get ugly with getting the cats together if it could be helped, and we were novices at this feline experience. We had tried a meeting of the two cats the day before, and that brief encounter consisted of BatGirl hissing and growling at Lucy, who stopped purring for the first time since we'd known her. In fact, Lucy actually frowned when BatGirl started her aggressive vocalizing; I don't know any other way to describe Lucy's expression. She remained quiet but seemed unafraid. Nevertheless, Mike and I were more than a little upset at BatGirl's behavior.

We had high hopes for the talents of Jan, the pet behaviorist. She arrived on a sunny day. We drank coffee and chatted for a while, and then she said, "Well, let's go meet the girls."

Mike brought Lucy downstairs. As soon as Jan saw her, she smiled and said, "Ah, you've got a Russian Blue. That's a sweet breed." We had no idea. We all fussed over Lucy for a while. Then BatGirl roused herself from her nap and joined us in the hallway. Always sociable to strange humans, she first rubbed on Jan. Then she spied Lucy. BatGirl froze, then began to slink in Lucy's direction, hissing and growling all the way. We stepped aside and watched as great big BatGirl tried to intimidate tiny Lucy. It was disturbing.

But Jan was unfazed. "The hiss is involuntary," she remarked.

"It is?" I said.

Jan nodded. "Cats hiss when they're scared."

"BatGirl's scared?" I said. "Of what?"

"She's scared of a strange cat," Jan said.

This had never occurred to me. "But BatGirl's so much bigger than Lucy," I said.

Jan shrugged. "BatGirl doesn't know that. So she's putting on a tough front. But she's scared of the kitten, I assure you. And here's the really good news," she added. "Lucy's not the least bit afraid of BatGirl. Check her out—she wants to play."

It was true. BatGirl's hissing and growling weren't scaring Lucy in the least. She even swatted at Bat-Girl's tail.

"I was concerned about these two at first since they're both females," said Jan, "but this kitten is a lover. She'll handle BatGirl just fine."

It took a week of strategic, supervised mixing of the two felines for brief periods, and then one day, Mike and I left the two alone together for the first time. When we returned a few hours later, we were met with quite a sight.

Mike walked in ahead of me and stopped at the back of an easy chair. As I wriggled out of my coat, he spoke to me quietly. "Come here and look."

I joined Mike and looked over the top of the chair. There on the seat was Bat-

71

Girl. She was spooned around tiny Lucy who was curled into a furry ball with her eyes squeezed shut. And BatGirl was grooming Lucy. Tenderly.

Mike and I grabbed hands and grinned stupidly at one another. BatGirl stopped her task and looked up at us. She had the gentlest expression on her face.

One always runs the risk of anthropomorphizing when trying to figure out what's going on in the mind of an animal, even one you know well. But it seemed to both Mike and me right then that BatGirl was thanking us for this fellow creature to share those many hours of being alone. BatGirl held our eyes a moment. Then she turned back to the work of grooming Lucy.

The girls, as we began calling them, got along fine after that day. Lucy had quite a calming effect on both the household and BatGirl. When I read up on the characteristics of the Russian Blue, I could see why.

Russian Blues were bred by Russian monks many centuries ago, using Siamese cats and French Chartreux cats. The Blues are shy and gentle. They walk on tiptoe like ballet dancers. They dislike loud noises. One of the myths of Russia is that soldiers draped the Blues over their shoulders to ride into battle with them. But I feel this would be highly unlikely for such a shy cat who hates noise and discord. I've always felt this myth was a way to lie about why the monks were breeding these cats in the first place—to wear their fur.

Blues need peace and quiet in the house. We could see this in the way Lucy deferred to BatGirl sometimes. It looked to us like Lucy just didn't want the hassle she was getting from our temperamental tortie. So she'd give in to keep the peace.

But the most striking evidence that we had a peacemaker in the house happened one day when Mike and I got into a shouting match about something. Mike and I both have expressive, strong personalities. We love and enjoy one another, but we'd unfortunately allowed ourselves to raise our voices at one another in our marriage more frequently than we should. On such occasions, the cats sometimes would simply leave the room.

One day, Mike and I were angry at one another. And we were both *right*. Just ask either of us! We followed each other from room to room, loudly making our points back and forth. Finally, in the kitchen, the accusations grew louder. We stood about four feet from one another volleying our stupid remarks . . . until we heard a steady staccato of meows. Loud meows. We stopped talking and looked down to see our shy blue cat marching back and forth between us, vocalizing loudly. She was loud enough that we heard her over ourselves. Back and forth, back and forth she went, meowing in a rhythm, as if to say, "Stop it, stop it, stop it!"

Did we stop? You bet we did. Mike said, "Is she doing this because of us?"

"I think so," I said.

We looked at each other and felt embarrassed. Then slowly, we both began to laugh.

Mike reached over and hugged me. He looked down at Lucy and said, "It's okay, Lucy." She looked at each of us, gave a final meow, and then strolled out of the room.

From then on, when voices started to rise, Lucy would run into the room and look at us and meow. And we would always calm down.

Do we have a more peaceful house because of a blue cat?

We do.

Was she meant to come to our house?

We believe she was. We saved Lucy from the elements, and in her own way, she saved us right back. She calmed us down, got us to play, got us to relax.

Blessed are the peacemakers indeed.

My Mother's Cat
Renie Burghardt

When my nineteen-year-old mother died, two weeks after giving birth to me, I inherited her cat, Paprika. He was a gentle giant, with deep orange stripes and yellow eyes that gazed at me tolerantly as I dragged him around wherever I went. Paprika was ten years old when I came into this world. He had been held and loved by my mother for all ten years of his life, while I had never known my mother. So I considered him my link to her. Each time I hugged him tightly to my chest, I was warmed by the knowledge that she had done so, too.

"Did you love her a lot?" I would often ask Paprika, as we snuggled on my bed.

"Meow," he would answer, rubbing my chin with his pink nose.

"Do you miss her?"

"Meow." His large, yellow eyes gazed at me with what I believed to be a sad expression.

"I miss her too, even though I didn't know her. But Grandma says she is in heaven, and she is watching over us from there. Since we are both her orphans, I know it makes her happy that we have each other." I would always say this, for it was a most comforting thought to me.

"Meow," Paprika would respond, climbing on my chest and purring. I held him close, tears welling in my eyes. "And it makes me so very happy that we have each other." Paprika's orange paw reached up and touched my face gently. I was convinced he understood me, and I knew I understood him.

You will always be lucky if you know how to make friends with strange cats.
Colonial American Proverb

At that time we lived in the country of my birth, Hungary, and I was being raised by my maternal grandparents. World War II had taken my young father away. As I grew, the war intensified, and soon we were forced to become migrants in search of safer surroundings.

In the spring of 1944, when I was seven, Paprika and I snuggled in the back of the wooden wagon as we traveled around our country. During the numerous air raids of those terrible times, when we had to scramble to find safety in a cellar, closet, or ditch, he was always in my arms, for I refused to go without him. How could I, when one of the first stories I was ever told as a child was that of my dying mother begging her parents to take care of her baby as well as her cat?

One day during the Soviet occupation of our country in the early spring of 1945, we emerged from a bunker where we had spent a terror-filled night. Paprika made friends with a young Russian soldier who treated him to tins of sardines because he reminded him of his own cat back in Russia. And always, during the trying times that persisted in our country, Paprika's love made things easier for me to bear. He was my comfort, my best friend.

By the fall of 1945, Grandfather had gone into hiding to avoid being imprisoned as a dissident by the new communist government. The solemn Christmas Grandmother and I expected turned into my worst nightmare when I awoke on Christmas morning to find Paprika, still curled up next to me, lifeless and cold. I picked up his body and held him close, sobbing uncontrollably. He was nineteen years old, and I was only nine.

"I will always love you, Paprika. I will never give my heart to another cat," I vowed through my tears. "Never, ever!"

My grandmother held me close, trying to console me. But my heart was broken on that terrible Christmas Day in 1945.

Christmas 1951 was our first Christmas in our wonderful new country, the United States of America. The horrors of war, the four years of hardship in a refugee camp, were behind us now, and a new life, filled with hope, lay ahead.

On that Christmas morning, I awoke to a tantalizing aroma wafting throughout the house. Grandmother was cooking her first American turkey. And one of the presents under the Christmas tree seemed alive, for it was hopping around to the tune of "Jingle Bells" playing on the radio. I rushed over, pulled off the orange bow, and took the lid off the box.

"Meow," cried the present, jumping straight into my lap and purring. It was a tiny, orange tabby kitten. When I looked into its yellow eyes, the vow I had made in 1945 crumbled away, and love filled my heart once again. I do believe my mother smiled down at us from heaven that Christmas Day.

The Writer and the Monk

Robert Benson

From time to time I will be on the road, reading from my books or leading retreats, and some budding writer will raise the question of how I have the discipline to get up so early each day and go to my studio and write.

I am tempted to tell them that I go to my studio before daybreak in the morning because it is simply the time of day that my brain is clear. The longer the day goes, the more clutter there is.

I am also tempted to tell them that I do not really have much discipline, but I do live with a cat.

It occurs to me just now that other than the fact that *discipline* and *cat* are both nouns, the two words have very little in common. Indeed, it may well be the first time that the two of them have ever actually been used in the same sentence.

We used to have three cats in our house, but we are down to one. We think of her as the caboose, so to speak.

We also refer to her as the Monk.

I am not actually a cat person.

I am not really even an animal person. I am actually afraid of anything larger than a cat, and any animal smaller than a cat gives me the creeps. Beyond that, whenever two or three cats are gathered, I begin to get a little nervous. Who knows exactly what is going on behind those sleepy little eyes?

I managed to avoid them for years.

Then the kind and sweet person with whom I fell in love revealed that she had two cats and that the whole business was pretty much a package deal. It is still the best deal that ever came my way, and I was smart enough to take it. And I am still more grateful than I ever imagined that I could be about anything. Especially when I remember one of our first evenings out when I spent an inordinate amount of time telling her how much I disliked cats.

It evidently made no difference to her. She is a cat person and she knew something that I did not.

There are some cats in our neighborhood that belong to the man who lives a couple of houses up the street from us. They pretty much live in our yard now; they just go visit him when they are hungry.

They seem to like our yard better than they like his. It could be because we have fences that keep dogs away and he does not. Or it could be that they prefer to nap in the sun at our house because they like the lawn chairs. It could be that they enjoy looking in the window at our cat and feeling superior about being able to have the run of the great outdoors. Invariably, there are one or two of them asleep by my studio whenever I go back and forth to the house.

When they first started showing up in our yard some years ago, I tried to explain to them that I am not a cat person.

I have offered the same explanation to the Monk, when I am trying to get her off my lap or out of my closet. All cats look at me as though they do not understand why it is I think that it is the person who decides whether or not he or she is a cat person.

In general, writers are rarely ever accused of hard work, and I am no exception, but my work, such as it is, seems at least more like work than what she does all day. All of my explanations of my non-cat-person status to the contrary, the cat who lives at our house considers us partners in my work. I do not recall making any sort of formal arrangement with her. She rarely asks for permission for anything.

She seems to have decided that her work is to make sure that I get up before dawn and go to the studio. Her work starts about ten the evening before.

There is a coffeepot in our house that has an alarm built into it so that I can make the coffee the night before and be able to have a cup before I am actually awake. If I had to wait for coffee until I was awake enough to make a pot, then I would be in trouble. Or at the very least, I would be in a bit of a snit each day before the day had even begun. I consider making the coffee the night before as a kind of preventative maintenance.

When I go into the kitchen to make the coffee in the evenings, the Monk will often come and sit on the kitchen table. The kitchen table is also known as Work Observation Post Alpha. She does not do any work, but she does like watching people who do. She takes up her post each evening to make sure I do it correctly and that I get it finished. Evidently there are nights when she is unsure as to how well I am performing the task, a task I have performed thousands of times while using the opposable thumbs that she so envies, because on those particular nights she will watch from the top of the refrigerator. The top of the refrigerator is known as Work Observation Post Beta.

When I have finished the coffee, I head down the hall to turn on the light at the end of the bookshelf. I do not like rising in the night to a dark house, so I leave a light on in the hall. I like to see where I am going if I have to get up, and I want to know where the Monk is so that she will not startle me in the night.

Before I go to bed, I go into the hallway to check to see if the cat's bowls are filled. If the coffee is not made so it is ready in the morning then I will be frantic in the morning, or agitated, at the very least. If the bowls are not filled, the cat will be frantic in the night and she will scratch at the bedroom door or walk on my pillow until I get up and remedy the situation. It does matter to me if she stays up all night sitting in the back hallway staring at her bowls and worrying that she will starve to death before dawn, but I have no desire to be awake half the night worrying with her when I know that she is in no danger of starving.

I keep my bedside clock set to wake me about fifteen minutes after the coffee has finished brewing in the morning. This is where the cat assumes her role as time management aide-de-camp to the poet.

Some mornings, I do not need the cat or the alarm to wake me up. I find myself, more and more often these days, awake well before the alarm and the coffee, lying in bed in the dark, waiting until it is a reasonable enough time to get up. One of my grandfathers told me that he used to lie in bed in the dark, waiting for the sun to come up so that he could get up. At the time, being a high school student, I thought that he must be crazy. Now I realize that he was only middle-aged, an age that roughly corresponds to the age that I am right now. I am not certain what I am in the middle of, though; it is not very likely that I will live to be 106.

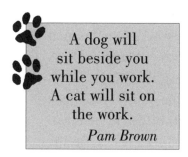

A dog will sit beside you while you work. A cat will sit on the work.

Pam Brown

But if I sleep through the alarm, or have set it for a later hour because we were up late the night before, or snooze button my way along for a while, the cat who lives at our house comes to wake me. She can be dead asleep somewhere in the house, dead asleep as only a cat can be, but she will hear the little click that the pot makes and then the bubbling noises, and she will smell the coffee and know that the poet is supposed to be up now.

She starts out sitting on the floor beside the bed, yapping away. She is actually the most talkative one in our house. I never really wanted to live in a house with a cat. How I ended up living with the most talk-ative cat on the planet is a mystery to me and seems like an unfair punishment. I have no idea what she is saying, but whatever it is, she is very vocal about it.

After a few minutes, if I have not crawled out of bed, she will make a couple of laps around my pil-low, carefully coming close to my ears but not quite touching them. In case there is an inquiry later, she wants to be sure that there is no trace of paw prints. (She does not feel this way about leaving traces of cat hair everywhere. My clothes invariably come back from the dry cleaners with her hair on them. I can take clothes to the cleaners, pick them up on the way to the airport, open my suitcase a thousand miles away, and there is evidence that the Monk had been there before I was.)

If, after some long stretch of time, like thirty-five to forty seconds—who knew that such a short period of time could seem like an eternity to an animal who sleeps all day—I have not gotten up, she will go into the hallway about eight feet from the bed and pound her paws on the closet door. I have never seen her do this, I am still in bed obviously, and the closet is around the corner, but I suspect that it looks like a modified version of that making biscuits thing that cats do when for some reason or another they remem-ber after all these years that they once had a mother, and they pretend that your lap will pass for mother and home. The banging on the closet door has that biscuit-making rhythm.

When I get up, she follows me to the kitchen and takes up Observation Post Alpha. When I go to the bathroom, she waits beside the door, and is not above making biscuits on the door if I am in there longer than she thinks is proper for a writer who has a deadline to meet. (How would she know about deadlines? She cannot even tell time, much less the date. She only knows it is October because we pile up clothes on the bed and pack for vacation.

So, when I am on the road and some budding writer raises the question as to how I have the discipline to get up so early each day and go to my studio, I nod very humbly and very sagely, and tell them it has taken years of steely determination, a steadfast commitment to the deep and honorable call of my vocation, and the unfailing and powerful grace of the One who made me. The One who happens to be the One who inexplicably made cats as well.

The Monk gets no credit. I am not a cat person, no matter what she says.

The Cat Who Would Eat Anything

Tracie Peterson

Our family has always been big on pets. We've had a variety in our day, but have settled for the time being on two cats and a dog. The cats include one gray tabby who is very fat and opinionated and one sleek black cat that flies from one end of the house to the other, taste-testing everything in between.

Safari Peterson came to us via the neighborhood kitten overpopulation. We adopted her, much to our older cat's disgust, and proceeded to play referee between the two. As Safari grew, we noticed she had a penchant for eating or chewing on just about anything. It definitely wasn't a safe hobby, but it seemed to be something we couldn't quite break her of, even for her own safety.

One morning as I was rushing around to take my husband to the airport, I noticed Safari wasn't feeling well. She was lethargic and from time to time would let out a miserable yawl.

"Looks like she's sick," my husband said, as he climbed over her with suitcase in hand. I nodded, figuring it was something minor and that it would pass.

"I'll check her out when I get home," I assured my husband, and we left for the airport.

When I returned, Safari was much worse. My youngest child, Erik, was quite worried about his kitten. He'd cared for her since she'd come into the family, and this was the first time we'd seen her sit still for more than thirty seconds. We took Safari to the vet and left her, as the office was too busy to see her immediately.

That afternoon, our world went completely upside down when the vet called to announce that Safari had ingested something he couldn't identify and that her stomach and bowels were hopelessly blocked. She would need surgery at an astronomical price, and even then, he said, the odds weren't good for survival.

Now I loved that cat as much as anyone in the family, but I had family elsewhere who were in extreme financial crisis. Spending this huge fee on a procedure that didn't look hopeful hardly seemed a wise choice. I wanted to be a good steward and also a conscientious pet owner, but there were no easy answers in this situation. My son was devastated. He could hardly bear the thought of losing his beloved Safari.

"Why is God doing this?" he asked me.

Stunned, I tried to think of a solid, inspiring answer. Nothing came to me, however. I was sad enough, all on my own, but seeing my child overwhelmed with grief was more than I could bear. "I don't think God is doing this to Safari," I told my son. "The cat ate things that weren't good for her, and now she's suffering the consequences."

"But God could have kept it from happening," Erik declared.

How many times had I said that myself about hundreds of other issues? God could have kept the 9/11 tragedies from happening. God could have kept my grandmother from suffering with Alzheimer's. God could have kept a lot of sadness and terrible things from happening to me. But he didn't.

"God could have kept it from happening," I finally agreed. "But he didn't. Does that mean he doesn't love you anymore? Does it mean you don't love him?"

My son stammered, "Well . . . no . . . I guess not. But . . . well . . . it's hard. I love that cat. I don't want her to die."

We sat down together, tears streaming down our faces. "I don't want her to die either, but sometimes these things happen."

"But why?" he asked.

I'd love to say that I had all sorts of wonderful wisdom for him, but I was so upset and so caught up in the moment, I could only shake my head and say, "Sometimes we don't get to know why."

Since the vet wanted to let Safari attempt to pass the mass of material, we had twenty-four hours in which to make a decision. Either we could pay the huge sum for surgery or we could put her to sleep. My son and I discussed the options, and no easy choices were to be found.

That afternoon my husband called, and I explained the situation to him. He was very close to Safari and hated to see her put to sleep, but since there were new family problems and financial complications for our daughter and her new family, he agreed we couldn't spend the extra money on surgery for a pet. So the decision was made. If Safari didn't get better, she'd have to be put down.

None of us slept well that night. The turmoil kept us tossing and turning until morning. Bleary-eyed, my son and I sat down to pray and wait for the call from the vet. When it finally came, the news wasn't good. She had not passed the blockage.

"We will have to put her to sleep," I explained to the vet. "We have a granddaughter who has just had multiple brain surgeries, and the bills are mounting. I can't in good conscience spend the money on the cat, when my family needs it to put food on the table." He informed me we'd need to come in and sign the release papers and say good-bye.

It was one of the hardest things I've ever had to do. We bid Safari good-bye, although she wanted nothing to do with either one of us. Her pain was pretty intense by this time.

Where's the Beef?

Cats cannot be vegetarians. Don't even try it; they'll die without animal flesh. Some dogs can do fine without consuming flesh, but not cats. One of the first things Mama Cat does is show her babies how to pounce and kill. And we humans think they're just playing . . .

My son and I went home to sit and mourn and think about the good times we'd had with our cat. We moped around the house and tried to work at our various tasks. Erik was still troubled by why this had happened. He told me he was praying about it, but that he didn't feel any better. My heart broke for him. I knew it was difficult to trust God at a time like this.

"Does God know how much it hurts?" my son asked.

"Yes," I assured him. "God knows exactly how much it hurts."

It wasn't long after this conversation that the phone rang. I assumed it would be my husband checking on us. Instead, I was surprised to hear the vet's voice.

"I decided," the vet began, "not to put Safari to sleep. I figured I'd perform the surgery for free and if she made it, I'd let you know and if she didn't, well, there'd be no harm done." He paused for a moment and left me with my heart in my throat. "I'm happy to say," he continued, "that the surgery was a success.

I found wound-up cording in Safari's stomach and believe it or not, a needle in her tongue. She's doing fine, however, and can go home tomorrow."

I nearly dropped the phone. We finished our conversation with me replying in a dumbfounded manner that I would wait for his call the next morning. I hung up the phone and went to find Erik. "You aren't going to believe this," I said, as I sat down with the teary-eyed boy.

"What?" he asked in complete dejection.

"That was the vet. He decided to operate on Safari for free. She's come through the surgery just fine, and she'll be able to come home tomorrow." I couldn't help but grin. "Isn't that the most incredible news?"

"It's God answering my prayer," he said softly. "He really does care."

I nodded. "Yes, he really does care. Even about silly little kittens."

God had taken Safari and her antics and helped my son's faith to grow tenfold. We knew it could have just as easily been a different story, but I believe God knew that my son needed a life lesson to increase his faith—to see God work in a seemingly impossible situation.

I'm happy to say that Safari Peterson is back home and quite well, although she doesn't seem as inclined to eat or chew on everything in sight. And best of all, my son has experienced falling into the hands of the living God, and it was indeed quite a fearful and wonderful thing.

The Manger Cat and His Mama

Paul Ingram

T hat calico's gone and had kits."

Granddad had a disgusted look as he sat in a kitchen chair to tug off his Wellingtons. "She's right by the hay winder of the shed. Them kittens may have to go. I got calves to put in there."

"I'll take hay in through the door," I said quickly. Granddad always found something to complain about, but I doubted he'd do violence to the family that had taken up residence in the old shed where we kept weaned calves—unless there was a blackie in the litter.

Granddad was Pennsylvania German stock, farmers who planted by the moon and hung mule shoes to catch good luck. Black cats brought the worst of bad luck, especially for themselves if Granddad got hold of them. Cats of other hues were tolerated. You couldn't milk them. They didn't lay eggs or produce rump roast. But they did keep rats and mice at bay, so they had their place in the general scheme of things.

That winter had been one to remember in Southern Indiana. Fence posts were buried in drifts. I'd had to load hay bales on my sled to pull out to where the shorthorns sheltered. We kept the newborn calves in the main barn into the spring, which was likely why the calico thought she could set up housekeeping in the manger of the shed, right by the opening where we threw in the hay. It was drafty, but otherwise a spacious nursery. When the window was open she even had a view.

Mama calico probably wondered why nobody had thought of having babies in a manger before.

My legs weren't long enough to see into the shed window, and galoshes made it a tough climb. It was doable if one wanted to see the new kittens bad enough. Just grab the sill, hook a foot on the door to the hay window, which hung down when the hatch was open. With a heroic pull up, I could climb to the sill and see down into the wood slats of the manger.

Except now the climb had an unforeseen hazard—a mad mama cat. As soon as a head showed up in the window, she took action.

"RAAWWRRRR!!! PSSSSSS!!! YOOOWWWW!!!"

The calico launched herself onto the sill, claws bared. But once she got there she had no one left to fight. She peered down from the ledge to where a seven-year-old human lay spread-eagled in the mud. She gave a final haughty hiss and disappeared back inside. Barn cats are not too sociable under the best of circumstances. These were not the best of circumstances.

However, if Mama Cat thought she had kept out the riff-raff, she hadn't heard about the five calves that were about to kick their heels into her domain and start poking wet noses and long tongues into the manger.

Granddad herded the calves into the shed, closed the door, and went his way, having entirely forgotten about the kittens. Evidently, it took about three minutes for cat and calves to get up close and personal. Bawls of pain echoed across the barnyard. The old

shed fairly shook as five startled young shorthorns stampeded against walls and then out the back door into their small fenced enclosure.

"They won't go back in, not even to eat," Granddad said at supper. He wasn't one to find humor in a lot of things, but he seemed amused as he pictured the five calves cowering before an eight-pound barn mama with a take-no-prisoners attitude.

Over the next days, life in the shed assumed a modicum of normalcy. The calves eventually were forced by hunger pangs to return to the manger. They took turns at the spot of hay farthest from the window, leaving the rest untouched. Eventually, Mama decided that she could live with visits from the seven-year-old human at the window, provided he brought bowls of milk and kept hands and feet out of reach of her claws and teeth.

At last I could finally take inventory of the tiny blind fluff balls that dozed in the cozy hay. There were four, two yellow tiger stripes, a calico, and one that was pure white. That white one was the attraction. I'd never seen an all-white cat before.

"Hi, little Snowball," I cooed and reached down, forgetting the unspoken but carefully enforced visitation rules. Nursing the latest scratches on my hand, I vowed that old mama cat had met her match.

She had to leave those kittens sometime.

On a sunny Sunday afternoon, I spied the warden heading into the barn. It was now or never. I sprinted toward the shed as soon as she was out of sight, climbed onto the sill, and slid down into the manger. I'd broken into the inner sanctum. A calf looked at me with big brown eyes full of concern. He was wondering who would feed him tonight if Mama Cat showed up about now. I lounged in the manger with the tiny white snowball nestled in my stocking cap, stroking its head.

Thus it happened that eyelids broke open, and Snowball got his very first look at the world, staring nose to nose with the biggest, ugliest mama he could imagine—me. Oddly, Mama had felt a lot snugglier when his eyes were still closed.

We can't choose our kin, and Snowball was faced with an awful truth about his family tree. He soon learned another hard fact about his mama, when another cat suddenly appeared in the window and started hissing.

Mama was a fraidy cat, who retreated over the side of the manger, scattering calves in all directions. But at least Snowball could snuggle for comfort into the cap that had been left behind.

Spring turned into summer vacation, and Mama Cat at last was able to move her brood to the safer confines of the barn. But she had continuing problems with her all-white son, who never really seemed to accept her authority. When she would take the kittens on a training expedition outside, Snowball would lag

cardinal and cat
keep close watch on each other
through black window screens

behind, looking for me. If he saw me heading out to play or do chores, he immediately abandoned the pretender and caught up with his "real" mama.

At least that's what Granddad said. "That kit imprinted on you," he explained. "He thinks you're his ma."

Granddad probably sympathized with Mama Cat. He had not enjoyed parenthood the first time around, and now he had to raise his grandson. He loved me in his way, but he didn't know quite what to do with a moody dreamer who sometimes wandered off in a haze, leaving the chores half done.

Meanwhile, Snowball learned to climb into the rafters and watch his mama turn the crank on the corn sheller or muck out the stalls. Snowball learned to hide and then pounce from the corncrib when his mama rode by on his stick horse. Despite this mama's failings, the manger cat loved unconditionally.

Alas, human-feline mother-son relationships can go only so far. Snowball grew to adulthood and began breaking the apron strings. He was, after all, still a barn cat, a wild hunter. As happens when children grow up and leave home, a more adult sort of respect and friendship formed. Snowball became a strongly muscled tom, with more than a hint of Siamese ancestry in his large blue eyes and darkening tail.

Sometimes he was nowhere to be seen for days at a time. Then suddenly there he was, tromping at my heels. Gradually I became aware that Snowball had stopped jumping out of hiding places to attack my

How's That for a Muse?

Charles Dickens's daughter had a deaf cat named Master who liked to perch on the author's writing desk. The cat enjoyed batting out Mr. Dickens's candle flame. When Dickens would re-light, Master would bat it out again.[4]

ankles. Then he was no longer there at all. I was an eight-year-old empty-nester, and it hurt.

"He's a tom," Granddad said. "Won't stay in one place. You'll not see him again."

It wasn't that Snowball haunted my consciousness, or that I kept a light on in the window. I was campaigning for a pony, although the chances did not look promising. Cats had a purpose. Ponies just ate and made manure. Granddad had a more colorful way of putting things, but that was the gist of it.

Then one day at evening chore time, I saw Snowball coming across the barnyard, the prodigal returning from a far land. He was limping, holding up a bloody paw. Worse, a big chunk of face was simply gone.

Grandma figured the bag balm ointment we rubbed on sore cow udders might be the thing, "but that cat will bite you if you hurt him. He's gone wild now."

Bite me? Snowball? The very idea.

And so I became a mama again and nurse to a battle-scarred, wayward son. He never bit or scratched, though the ministrations must have caused pain. He still couldn't come into the house. Piglets in distress occasionally reached the kitchen for care, but no cat ever crossed that social barrier. Nevertheless, Snowball had a soft box on the porch, and for a few days took his meals in bed. He never gave explanation or apology for his long absence, but the quiet bond was still there. He'd stay this time.

"You cain't keep 'im," said Granddad. "He'll follow his nature."

As usual, Granddad proved maddeningly right, but not before Snowball and his mama had a few months to come to terms with their differences. A succession of birds, mice, and chipmunks were dropped at Mama's feet by a proud son. It wasn't quite the same as a Hallmark card, but the sentiment was appreciated.

Then Snowball just wasn't there.

One year passed, two, three.

I was now in seventh grade in the midst of a full-blown pubescent identity crisis. It was a tough transition for a loner country boy with a tendency toward depression.

On a particularly bad day, I was again fantasizing about the option of death, as I shoveled winter corn out of the wooden storage crib. A movement caught my eye, and I looked up into the rafters. An enormous white tomcat with blue eyes and a scarred face looked down. He didn't move. He just watched. I never saw him again, but that's okay. His last visit was a reminder that we mamas have to go on. We never know when we may be needed once more.

Frankie,
the Guardian Cat

Alyce McSwain

It was the Saturday before Easter, 1981, and we were at the animal shelter to pick out a kitten for our four-year-old daughter, Jennifer, and our twenty-month-old son, Robert. Sitting way back in a cage full of kittens was a tiny, gray, wide-eyed ball of fur meowing desperately. I liked him immediately. *He has a perfect "M" on his forehead for McSwain*, I mused.

Back in the car, I asked Jennifer if she wanted to name him Dusty, or Smokey, in keeping with his color, but she adamantly announced that she was naming him after her father, Douglas Franklin McSwain. "Okay," I said, "but we're calling him Frankie!" He curled up in my lap and started sucking on my finger.

Frankie must have been too young when he was taken from his mother because he would spend hours lying on Jennifer's chest "nursing" her fingers or ear lobes. But strangely enough, his main attachment was to our baby. He followed him around like a dog even though Robert carried him by his head or tail. When he had enough, he would escape behind the gate in front of the stairs. Robert was a mischievous

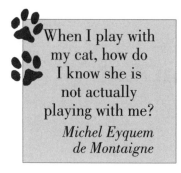

> When I play with my cat, how do I know she is not actually playing with me?
>
> *Michel Eyquem de Montaigne*

baby. He would hide from me and not answer when I called. But since the cat was always with him, I would just listen for a meow. One time I found them together in my bedroom closet. Robert was busy trying to brush the cat's teeth. The cat never put out his claws but sat limply in the toddler's lap spitting out toothpaste.

We lived on the edge of a man-made lake. It had been dug out, and it dropped off sharply at the edge. There was no wading in the water. We had a fenced-in yard for protection. One sunny day, I was hanging out sheets on the line, and the children were playing in the yard. I took my eyes off them for a minute to untangle a sheet. When I looked around, the gate was open and Jennifer was sitting on the little bridge over the stream that lay between our house and the lake.

"Where's Robert?" I screamed. She shrugged her shoulders. I dashed across the bridge and looked both ways. No toddler. I started running along the path to the right. Suddenly, I stopped and screamed, "God, help me find my baby!"

Instant calm came over me, and I heard these words clearly in my head: *Call your cat.* "Frankie!" I cried. There was dead silence. And then I heard that familiar meow coming from way behind me. I whirled around and saw the cat coming out of the bushes that lined the lake. I ran to the spot and there on the very edge of the lake was Robert leaning precariously over the water. I scooted down the slope and grabbed him with Frankie at my heels. I picked up the baby and the cat, crying and thanking God all the way home for sending us this pound cat to save my baby's life.

When Frankie matured, he started wandering, and one time he was gone several days. I called the vet, who said, "After ten days, you can consider him gone for good." I tried to break the news gently to Jennifer that Frankie had probably gone off and found another loving family, but she refused to listen. Each night, when she said her prayers, she told God that she wanted her cat back. She didn't ask. There was no doubt in her mind that her prayer would be answered.

The children were asleep one night two weeks after Frankie went missing when Doug and I heard an awful screeching at the door. I opened it, and a scraggly, dirty gray cat came in. I ran and woke Jennifer and said, "Your cat has returned." She just looked at me and replied, "I told you God would bring him home." And she rolled over and went back to sleep.

Frankie continued to adore Robert. As our son grew older, we had him tested for allergies and found out that he was highly sensitive to cat dander. The doctor recommended that we get rid of the cat. I told him that I would never part with the cat because he had saved my son's life. Robert took shots and eventually built up an immunity. In his later years, the cat even slept with Robert. Frankie would wake Robert up each morning in time for school.

When Frankie was almost eighteen, Robert went off to college. Frankie sat in front of our son's bedroom door and cried every day. I would rock him and tell him that Robert would be home soon. One morning that October, Frankie did not come to the door and greet us. We searched and finally found him under his favorite bush in the backyard. His job of guarding Robert was finished. Frankie simply died in his sleep.

We took the cat to our cabin at the lake and buried him in the backyard. Our dog, Marble, usually a very quiet animal, saw us through the screen door, standing in a circle around Frankie's grave. Marble howled and railed against the door until one of us let her out. She darted up the hill and lay down on the grave and would not move. We had to carry her back in the house with us. When four years later the dog died, we buried her next to Frankie, our guardian cat.

The Cat Who Loved Chemo

Sue Buchanan

I have been owned by many cats in my lifetime, some whose names I've forgotten. Some I named childish names like Baddie and Goodie because they were bad or good; and in fact I was a child.

At a very young age, I strolled the block with my cat, Smokey the Pirate Don Derk of Don Day, both of us dressed to the nines—me in high-heeled shoes with holes that let my toes poke out, Mother's old lace blouse that came to my ankles, a wide-brimmed felt hat with a veil to the chin, black gloves with rhinestone cuffs, and an animal around my neck that bit its own tail. I was known as Mrs. Vandertweezers at the time, and for days at a time I wouldn't answer to Sue, only to Mrs. Vandertweezers. Elegant lady that she was, I felt her wardrobe rivaled that of any Hollywood star or even that of the Queen of England.

Her regal companion, Smokey the Pirate Don Derk of Don Day, rode on his back in the doll buggy dressed in a doll dress and bonnet as Mrs. V strolled the block. Past Mrs. Eubanks's house, past the Liebles', past the convent, and past the Catholic school to Sacred Heart Catholic Church (which was as far as she was allowed to go) and back again.

"Hello, dahling!" she said to everyone.

"Everyone" was mostly the sisters walking back and forth between church, school, and convent. Sometimes Mrs. Vandertweezers and Smokey the Pirate were invited into the convent for a visit and some ice cream. Once they actually made a little turn through the foyer of the church, but they left hurriedly when Father Cuthbert came toward them—his robes flying—with his eye on Smokey the Pirate Don Derk of Don Day.

Going to that magnificent church and having a string of those nice tiny black beads, doing the little curtsy, and being slightly mysterious was more than a little appealing to Mrs. Vandertweezers. She gave Catholicism strong consideration. Naturally, she couldn't possibly become a nun because then she couldn't be Mrs. Vandertweezers or enjoy her lavish wardrobe!

After Smokey there was Agamemnon, the smartest cat ever to own me. He got his name from *The Four Little Kittens*, a book I still have after all these years. The book begins: "Once upon a time, there were four little kittens. Their names were Buzz, Fuzz, Suzz, and Agamemnon." It ends: ". . . when their mother tucked

Agamemnon into bed, she remembered he was the youngest and had tried the hardest. So she gave him an extra kiss on the tip of his nose." My mother never let me kiss Agamemnon or my other cats on the nose or anywhere else. She said I would get a horrible disease. (Today I kiss my cat and wonder what Mother would think if she knew.)

Among other manifestations of intelligence, Agamemnon could turn the piano light on and off. He would use his claws to grip the pull-chain. On and off it would go—a wonderful distraction when I was supposed to be practicing.

I still have the newspaper clipping that tells of Agamemnon's disappearance and my letter to the Great Scott, our local radio personality, telling him my "best friend" was lost and would he please help find him. I didn't mention that my best friend was a cat until the very last line.

Great Scott read my letter over the air, and sure enough, a listener heard my plea and discovered the "guest" in his home was not just an ordinary stray. He should have known! Strays don't stretch out over half the length of the buffet without touching a single piece of crystal. Strays don't sit by the refrigerator, looking at it through half-closed eyes, then look at you in the same manner, back and forth until you say, "Okay, okay, I'll feed you!" And strays do not turn lights on and off. The man brought Agamemnon back, and he lived happily with us for many more years.

I went on to have more cats, and twenty years ago, there was Ya. When I think about chemotherapy, I remember Ya, my friend and companion during my dreary months of treatment for breast cancer. It's hard to believe it was so long ago. But first, more about Ya.

We think of our beloved cat Ya every year at Christmas when I pull the Christmas tree skirt out of the box and admire its beauty. It wasn't easy, gluing on all those pieces of felt and tiny little sequins—ladies dancing, calling birds, French hens. Right over there by the swans a'swimming is a faded brown spot. We look at it each year and say, "Oh, that's where Ya threw up, God rest his soul!" A tear comes to the eye.

We got Ya when the girls were little. Grandma had just been to Greece and heard the ladies there calling their cats: "Yata . . . yata." So the girls named this cat Ya. He made the move with us to Nashville and grew old and bored (not bored because of Nashville . . . just bored).

One of Ya's claims to fame was that he was true to a comment of Theophile Gautier: "He loved books, and when he found one open on the table, he would lie down on it, turn over the edges of the leaves with his paw; and after a while, fall asleep, for all the world as if he had been reading a fashionable novel." Each week, my husband, Wayne, and I read the Sunday newspaper, and as we finished with the various parts, we tossed them to the floor and waited.

Sure enough Ya would walk around on each section, sometimes stopping on the funnies or the want ads to take a bath, then curl up on the Sunday Showcase for a long afternoon nap. Always the Sunday Showcase—that is until I was executive of the week in the

Business Perspective. That day he skipped the funnies and the want ads, didn't even glance at sports, fashions, or showcase. He went straight to the Business Perspective, looked at my picture, read the article, then chose that exact place to take his nap. We even snapped pictures to prove it.

I hate to say this out loud, but Ya loved chemotherapy. He seemed happiest during my year of bad health, and he made my life more bearable.

Treatment began five days after my mastectomy while I was still in the hospital. I've come to believe that beginning so quickly was an incredibly wise decision on the part of my oncologist. "Begin now!" he said. "Remember those cells are reproducing themselves at a staggering rate. We need to catch them before they get a head start on us." It must have worked, as I'm alive these many years later. The program he set up for me was pretty standard at the time. It called for bombarding my body with chemicals for two weeks and then allowing it to revitalize for two weeks.

God made the cat in order to give man the pleasure of petting the tiger.

Unknown

Because of everything I'd heard about chemotherapy, I had a mind-set against it from the beginning. I expected it to make me sick. The doctor's office smelled like a chemical factory, and the aftertaste in my mouth was how I imagined dry cleaning fluid would taste. Right from the beginning, I fussed and stewed about this yucky stuff. In my mind, I called it every bad name I could think of. I regarded the visits to the doctor's office a nuisance. "A ridiculous waste" was my label for the time I had to reserve for recuperation after treatment. It was ridiculous that I had to put up with this interference in my busy schedule.

After a couple of months of fighting against everything chemo represented, I forced myself to change my attitude. One day as I waited at the doctor's office, it came to me: *I shouldn't be fighting this. Chemo is good and could be my cure. I must accept this medicine into my body with thanksgiving, trusting it will work for me and make me well.*

From that day forward, I didn't mullygrub about chemo. I waltzed into that little room, pulled off my clothes, put on the sticky little bolero, raised my hands to God, and thanked him. "Dear God, take the medicine and put it where it will do the most good," I'd say, ". . . and thank you, God. Thank you from the bottom of my heart."

Later, at home, I began to spend more time thanking God, not only for the medicine and the health professionals but for my husband who enjoyed making my life easy, my daughters who loved me dearly, and my friends who supported me in every way.

One of those friends gave me a colorful book called *The Human Body*—a children's book; I began incorporating its illustrations into my prayers. "This is a picture of a healthy brain, Lord. Help mine to be healthy and free from cancer." I did the same with the pictures of liver, lungs, and bones, the likely places breast cancer would metastasize. The pictures certainly didn't help God. He knew what my insides looked like. They helped me.

The first two or three months chemo only made me tired, and I went home and slept the afternoon away after treatment. I felt progressively worse each month, eventually throwing up at the very thought of the procedure. Each time I went for chemo, Wayne took me and picked me up. He offered to go in with me, but I knew he needed to be at the office; I also knew sometimes a doctor tends to "talk around" a patient when a spouse is present. Instead, I wanted a strong partnership between my doctor and me.

My appointment was at one o'clock in the afternoon, allowing me a productive morning in the office. Afterward Wayne would take me home and turn me over to Ya for the afternoon. Ya would curl into the curve of my body, and we would both sleep the afternoon away. The nausea continued to become worse. It hit late in the afternoon and I was sick—so sick—through the evening and into the night. Ya was tolerant. When I was in the bathroom, he took the opportunity to have his evening meal and his bath; but each time I returned to bed, he was waiting to cuddle and comfort.

On the day of my treatment, I must have looked and felt worse than my childhood cat Agamemnon did after he'd been out for two or three days and nights at a time, doing whatever it is tomcats do! He used to drag his big, old, yellow body through the door, turn his ears back at the food we offered, flop down, and with all the energy he could muster, lick his wounds—sometimes bloody; once with part of an ear missing—and give us a look that said, "Do not disturb!" Then he'd sleep the day away.

On the day after my treatment, I'd drag myself out of bed, turn my nose up at food (the people version of cats turning their ears back), and lick my wounds. The nausea came now and then but lessened as the day progressed. Eventually, I'd try a piece of toast with a tiny bit of peanut butter.

My yellow cat stuck with me through it all. For a while even after my treatment was over, he would meet us at the door, lead us to the bedroom, leap on the bed, and look at us expectantly. He seemed to be saying, "Come on, let's be sick some more!"

One day Ya didn't come when we called. We searched the woods—he never went far. Every day after that, we hoped as we came up the drive. Finally I knew he was gone.

I still miss Ya and hope his end was peaceful. I would have liked to comfort him as he comforted me so many times.

Cat Lady

Thora Wease

Every neighborhood had one. You remember. A cat lady who lived alone but had dozens of cats. Dogs were seldom the preferred choice for pet companionship *en masse*. Perhaps dogs were too busy, or noisy, or expensive, or attracted too much attention from the local licensing authorities. I don't ever remember a "Dog Lady" but our town certainly had a Cat Lady. I would walk by the infamous house marveling at the cats perched on every window ledge, vigilant sentries stoically poised in motionless duty to her majesty: Queen Cat Lady.

As children we used to count them as best we could: four tabbies, the dingy white one, the scary black one, three calicos, and the one we called Double-o-Three because it had only three legs. For some reason we were fascinated with this menagerie and their matriarch. Secreted in the bushes across the street we would watch the morning ritual with reverence. Cat Lady would come onto the porch with saucers of milk, and the horde would converge eagerly but with respectful dignity. Each would pay homage, in turn, briefly rubbing against ancient legs with tail raised high in salute to their benefactor. She knew them all by name, and some would chat with her between sips of milk. When the milk was gone they would retire, bidding their queen a grateful bow and meow.

It was after the others had gone that Bushbaby would peer out from the prickly bush nearest the porch and timidly make his way up the steps. They had an agreement, Bushbaby and the queen: she would put down a little saucer just for him and then pretend not to see him. There were rules. She would talk to him in a soft baby voice while he was drinking and his tail said that it pleased him. Touching was out of the question. Once Cat Lady tried to renegotiate the contract by stroking the matted head and was chastised by a primal scream so fearful that it sent us screaming home to our own mothers.

We never saw Cat Lady touch Bushbaby again until the day he didn't come up the stairs and she went into the prickly bush after him. She turned toward us holding the stiff cat, her arms bloody from the prickers on the bush. We watched stone silent as Cat Lady wrapped Bushbaby in a towel and then put him in a box. Ignoring the now dry streaks of blood on her arms, Cat Lady dug a hole beneath the prickly bush and there she deposited the box with the gentleness of a mother. Overcome by

The Eyes Don't Necessarily Have It

We assume cats have excellent vision, but some cat vision is good, some not so much. They do see well at night and in semi-light. But cats are a little nearsighted, and they literally cannot see anything directly under their noses. The cat's best sense is the olfactory one. This probably explains their love of your unwashed clothes in the laundry basket. Those clothes smell tantalizingly like you. Ever see your cat sniff something at length, then open its mouth for a moment? Cats actually have a second organ for smelling especially interesting odors— the Jacobson's organ, located in the roof of the mouth.

the sadness of it all, we became chief mourners at the funeral of Bushbaby. Our wailing and heartbroken sobs drew attention from across the street; her knowing gaze was almost grateful as she wiped sweat from her brow but didn't bother to wipe the tears streaming from her eyes. She was not mourning her loss alone. It was too much for us. We abandoned our hiding place, we even avoided her street, but for a long time after that every cat reminded me of Bushbaby's funeral.

The years passed. I studied Egyptians and their love affair with the cat and I thought about Cat Lady. I studied psychology and the need of humans for companionship and thought about Cat Lady. I studied religion and the concept of unconditional love and I thought about Cat Lady. I studied English and discovered that Ernest Hemingway broke the cat-collector gender barrier with a score of cats, to whom he left a hefty chunk of his estate, and I thought about Cat Lady. A few years ago, I heard that fire destroyed her home, and Cat Lady was sent to a nursing home, which of course, did not allow even one cat. She promptly died, much to everyone's surprise . . . except mine.

I share my life with one feline. Mr. Phil was less of a stray than a fur-person looking to improve his circumstances, and it was my good fortune that he found my accommodations suitable. It has not been without compromise. I have added dog-owner-like walks to my daily regimen; Mr. Phil, for his part, has submitted with dignity to the harness and leash. Our neighbors have become accustomed to seeing us and always address him by name while I, on the other end of the leash, retain my anonymity.

But it is on those rare occasions, encountering a new child, that Mr. Phil hoists his twenty-pound countenance upright like a giant orange-striped pear and, waving a mitten-paw, conducts the symphony of delighted squeals. I did not instruct Mr. Phil; he came with these abilities and tendencies. It was not until yesterday that I discovered that I am known among the children on our route. It came from the bushes, as all truly important proclamations do: "Here comes Cat Lady!" The child's voice propelled from the hedgerow, catapulting me back to my childhood.

Me? No. No!

Apparently, a vast number of felines are not required to make a cat lady. The thought of it haunted me. What exactly makes a cat lady? What makes *me* a cat lady?

I have seen the clever tomes ingratiatingly attributing one's sum total of knowledge to a dog, or cat, or potbellied pig but, save the importance of naps, I have learned little from Mr. Phil. However, I have learned a great many things from Cat Lady. She was a wealth of inspiration: Cat Lady was accessible. She was generous. She asked nothing in return but graciously accepted her cats' unique expressions of thanks. She never treated the challenged Double-o-Three any differently than she did the others. She respected Bushbaby's need for extra personal space but wasn't afraid to risk rejection to let him know more attention was available, if desired. She used their names and looked them in the eye. She was someone they could depend on. There was always room for one more at her table. She recognized the importance of combining dignity with charity. She didn't let public detractors sway her from her mission. She didn't let the absence of human love in her life make her bitter, but instead she took that wealth of untapped love and showered it on the unloved. I regret never getting to know her but after some postmortem research discovered her name was Martha.

In a cat's eye,
all things belong
to cats.
English proverb

I am small scale compared to Martha, and I still have lots of contact with people, but to the little ones in the bushes I am Cat Lady and all that the title confers. In this age where it is increasingly difficult to meet people and even more difficult to maintain deep relationships, our greatest risk is forgetting how to give and accept love. Fortunately, the fur people in our lives keep us in touch with our core of loving. If I am ever fortunate enough to find a human being as my companion, he will undoubtedly be someone who has kept in the practice of giving and accepting love with the assist of a fur person.

In the meantime I will enjoy Mr. Phil and wear the crown of Cat Lady with pride.

Iffy
Linda Shands

My new friend, Bertha, eased herself onto the sofa while I unloaded groceries in her kitchenette. A skinny black-and-white cat crept from behind the refrigerator and leapt onto the cushion beside her. Bertha reached out and stroked its head.

"This is Iffy," she said, her face wreathed in a smile. "She came to me a year ago." Bertha lowered her voice. "I call her Iffy because she's an 'it,' you know."

I laughed. Then Bertha grew serious and looked me square in the eyes. "God sent her to me."

I had met Bertha a few months before on the city bus. A short, stocky lady with a bent back and twisted hands, she nevertheless wore flawless makeup and was dressed to the nines. She had seemed pleased when I chose the seat next to her, and we chatted. She spoke in a heavy European accent when she told me,

"For years I worked in fashion sales. Now I volunteer at the hospital."

In spite of her physical disabilities and pain, Bertha was an active, cheerful person. I learned she had grown up in Denmark. During the war, her family helped Jews escape the holocaust. Her fiancé was killed in the street outside her home. Later she married an American and came with him to the United States. He did the shopping and cooking while she pursued her career at a major department store.

Then her husband passed away. She had no other family, so as her physical condition deteriorated and her ability to work declined, her funds dwindled rapidly. When I learned she was living on oatmeal, coffee, and ice cream, I offered to help her shop. Stocking her fridge with milk, fruit, and frozen dinners was a blessing for both of us.

"Just let me get us some coffee," she said now, "and I will tell you about Iffy."

I sat across from her and sipped a thick European brew. Iffy had darted under the bed and did not reappear as Bertha began her story.

"When Walter passed on," she said, "I sold the house and moved to an apartment with our two little dogs." Her eyes clouded. "They were my life, but then I had a stroke and could not take care of them.

"When I came out of the hospital," she continued, "I was alone, and my money was gone. I had a little business knitting caps and baby things. Six hours a day I would work, but the arthritis got so bad I could

A Surprise Confession

As many Floridians know, American novelist Ernest Hemingway was a friend to cats in his home in Key West. Most of his cats were polydactyls, meaning they had extra toes on their paws. Their descendents—also polydactyls—still live in the late author's Florida house, supported by Hemingway's estate. Hemingway once remarked, "I have just one consolation in my life. My kitty."[5]

not knit anymore." She rubbed her twisted hands. "My friends helped, but they were busy. They said I must move and let the government take care of me."

Her lips trembled as she told me, "I could not bear it. The shame, you know." She raised a hand to silence my protest. "One day, I woke up and did not want to live."

I fought back tears as Bertha relayed the events of that day. How she had struggled out of bed at noon. How she selected a bottle of painkillers from a shelf crowded with prescription medications and counted them out, wondering how many it would take. How she had swallowed only the first two when the phone rang.

"Let me tell you," she said, "that phone scared me so bad I spilled pills all over the sink. I didn't want to answer, but it rang and rang." She placed her hand on her chest. "Something in here told me it was important." Her eyes softened as she glanced toward the bedroom where two white paws stuck out from under the bed.

"I found a cat," her friend on the phone had said. "She's been abused. She needs a quiet home and lots of love. Will you take her?"

Bertha chuckled. "I knew nothing about cats, but I couldn't let the poor thing die." Her mouth hardened, remembering. "They brought her over that same day. She was scared of her own shadow. I was so mad. What had they done to her? For two weeks she hid under the bed. I bought her toys and coaxed her to eat." Bertha's grin lit up the room. "She finally let me touch her. Now, when I've been out, she meets me at the door and scolds me for leaving her."

Iffy now appeared in the bedroom doorway. She crept past me to settle with a soft thump in Bertha's lap. Bertha stroked the silky fur. "We need each other. I think God knew that."

I smiled. "Yes, Bertha," I said, "I'm sure God knew that all along."

One More Time

Terri Castillo-Chapin

Thomas Chapin was a hard-playing, spirited saxophonist-flautist who performed jazz on big outdoor stages and in concert halls and tiny clubs all over the world. He was an original who often said, "Music is my first love." The critics called him "raucous" because he played with such intense physical energy and prowess, sometimes "using yells, roars, and howls to charge his performances."

Yet when it came to animals, no one could be softer or gentler than Thomas. Furry and feathered creatures especially delighted him. They were, shall we say, his second love. So it is not surprising that, in 1997, when he suddenly fell ill at the age of thirty-nine, an animal—a black-and-white stray kitten named Moi—became a comfort and strength to him in his final days.

As a child in Manchester, Connecticut, Thomas had grown up around cats: Boots, an all-black cat with white paws; Felicia, a regal angora with a huge plume tail; and Thomas's favorite, Charlie, a plump, gray-and-white tiger (named after the legendary saxophonist Charlie Parker). Charlie slept at the foot of Thomas's bed during his teen years.

I remember, when I first met Charlie at the home of Thomas's parents, how he had a strong and intelligent presence, an independent air. By that time, Thomas was living in New York City, pursuing a career in jazz, and we were dating. I was struck by how dear this cuddly creature was to him. Often we would arrive at his parents' house and the first thing Thomas would do was rush inside, drop his bags, and call out, "Charlie! Charlie!" Thomas lit up when Charlie appeared. One day when we visited, his mother spoke softly upon our arrival. "Tom," she said, "Charlie was sick and had to be put down." Thomas's head dropped to his chest and, in silence, he walked to his bedroom and didn't come out until the next morning.

Shortly after, we were married and lived in a cozy one-bedroom apartment in Queens, New York. By then, Thomas had left a well-known big-band orchestra to form his own group, writing and performing his own compositions. He was happily making a dream come true. "I don't want to play, I must play," he said, explaining that music was his fate rather than a choice. Thomas was deeply spiritual, and he thanked God for the privilege of being able to do what he loved. Through the late eighties and nineties, he became widely known for his work in modern jazz with a trio that included a drummer and a bassist. Through his record label, he was regularly touring the United States, Canada, Europe, and Japan, making records and gaining a following.

And animals? They were still a steady component of his life. While our working schedules didn't allow us to have cats, we were able to have two perky, yellow cockatiels, Tweeter and Pai. Thomas taught them words and, by whistling, he would imitate their irrepressible melodies and squawks.

As for cats, they still surrounded Thomas in the streets, darting in and out of alleys, at rehearsal spaces, at friends' homes, and on the road. He'd find them, play with them, and adopt them on the run. He even wrote and recorded tunes that captured the spirit of the animals he had known and loved.

Thomas was now busier than ever, at the top of his form. He was cited as "one of the few jazz musicians of his generation to exist in both the worlds of the downtown, experimentalist scene and mainstream jazz." Then on one trip abroad, he unexpectedly fell ill. When he returned home, he was diagnosed with leukemia. This was stunning news, but even that could not keep him down. He brought that raucous playing spirit, along with his faith, to battle the disease. During his many months undergoing chemotherapy, he inspired his own doctors and nurses. He wanted to be back onstage playing, doing what he loved.

After three months of enduring some of the most punishing days a human being could suffer, he was in remission and returned home. It was Good Friday. We both had so much to be thankful for, and it was one of our happiest times. While a long road still lay ahead, the doctors said, "Live your life. Play music." In between treatments, Thomas performed again in clubs and at outdoor summer concerts. At home, he read, listened to music, and occasionally tried to compose, surrounded by the cockatiels who cheered him and whose sounds and antics inspired in him fresh ideas.

Then at the end of summer, he

received discouraging news. The leukemia was back and there was little more the doctors could do. "I want to live," Thomas said to me. "I want to grow old with you. I want to play again."

We mustered all of our energy and looked into alternative therapies and clinical trials. These were not the easiest of days, yet we had so much: our faith, our families and friends, each other. Thomas maintained a rigorous spirit and optimism. These days he wasn't playing music onstage; the instrument he now played was himself. His generosity, courage, and humor were the notes coming out of him, and people—even strangers—were attracted to him. Often doctors and nurses called or stopped by the house to say hello, and former hospital roommates would phone him.

You can't look at a sleeping cat and be tense.

Journalist Jane Pauley

Between the new treatments and outpatient visits, Thomas spent most days in the sunny, back room of our apartment—his music room—that overlooked a neighbor's small garden. We had to ask Thomas's father to come and take the cockatiels away until Thomas was better. His father took the birds to a children's museum near their home in Connecticut where they were welcomed and cared for.

It was late fall and the days were shorter. The house was quiet without the birds. Treatments were continuing. Thomas was frail. One day I found him in the music room, sitting with the saxophone on his lap, tears in his eyes. "I just want to play again," he sighed. And then, as if knowing some truth that hadn't yet registered with me, he said, "I want to play one last time."

As the weeks passed, I began to feel the weight of the illness overtaking all of our long, hard efforts. I could see Thomas's fatigue; this was to be one of his most challenging periods. Yet, he wouldn't give up. The desire to play music again fueled his fight.

One day Thomas stood at the window overlooking a neighbor's house. "Come quickly," he called. I ran over and stood next to him, looking out. He pointed to a small black-and-white kitten we'd never seen before frolicking in the garden. The energetic darling was making such a fuss, jumping high to catch a squirrel scampering up a tree trunk, darting between flower bushes and having a . . . well . . . raucous time in the garden. Thomas was mesmerized, laughing at the entertainment. The next few mornings it was showtime for the cat, and Thomas was the audience. Afterward, Thomas would return to his piano and play with renewed concentration.

One morning Thomas got dressed and said, "Let's go outside and find the kitten."

"I don't think so," I replied. "You know stray city cats aren't very friendly."

But Thomas was already out the door, and I was trailing behind him. When he reached the neighbor's yard, the kitten—from nowhere—came bounding into his arms. Thomas just laughed as the kitten nibbled up against his face. It was as if these strangers were old friends.

Day after day, Thomas would go out to greet the kitten. One day he learned that our building superintendent had adopted the kitten and let her wander in the basement. That became the new rendezvous for Thomas and the kitten, now named Moi by our super's children. "We don't know where she came from," the kids said while feeding her milk.

The leaves started falling off the trees, then came Christmas and blustering snows. Thomas was walking more slowly now, but having his friend in the basement somehow made things easier. Moi was becoming a very special presence to both of us, and we talked about keeping her ourselves. But life was too erratic now; we first had to get Thomas's health and strength back.

It was February; the snow lay packed under minus zero temperatures. A year had passed since Thomas had fallen ill. Musicians from his home state planned a benefit concert for him in his parents' hometown. For weeks the event was written about in the local papers and announced over the radio. By now Thomas had grown quite weak. "I want to attend the concert," he told me and the doctors. They weren't sure that being three hours away from them was a good idea. But on the day of the concert, the doctors agreed to let him go.

Thomas, who had not been anywhere in months, was overjoyed. A friend came to drive us. Before we left the apartment, Thomas tucked into his bag the silver flute his parents had given him for graduation. He went downstairs to see Moi. She wiggled playfully under his embrace. "Good-bye, Moi," he said, hugging her close. "You be a good girl while I'm gone."

We left the concrete sidewalks and dense surroundings of our city dwelling and breathed in the fresh, cool air and wide, open spaces of the approaching countryside. Arriving in the Connecticut neighborhood of his childhood, Thomas perked up at the sight of the familiar scenery: snow-covered fields where he cross-country skied as a child, hills and woods full of tall trees, winding trails, and icy brooks. He had hiked there often and found treasured solitude among the birds, the squirrels, and the deer. When we arrived at his parents' house, he didn't go in immediately, but walked on the frozen ground and among the trees in the yard. He stopped and listened to the song of a bird. I think Thomas could have stood there forever.

We were in the kitchen sipping hot tea with his family when Thomas's father asked, "Would you like to see the cockatiels over at the children's museum?"

"Yes!" Thomas cried, and jumped up to get his jacket.

We drove over. It had been more than six months since we had seen the birds. When Thomas put his face to the cage, Tweeter and Pai began squawking and flapping their wings excitedly. They recognized him! He called out their names, gave his signature whistle, and they answered. A little improvised concert was

Who's Training Whom?

It's an age-old question: Can cats be trained? Or is it true what they say—dogs have masters, cats have staff? Yuri Kuklachev of Russia's Moscow Cats Theatre travels worldwide with twenty domestic cats who actually perform tricks. It should be no surprise to cat lovers that this is the only domestic cat circus in the world. So how *does* Kuklachev train? He claims he doesn't; rather, he is an observer of cats and how each one likes to play. Since cats are not only playful but also highly ritualistic, these very games become circus tricks. So that Kuklachev's cats can adjust to the noise of a live audience, they "train" to recordings of applause.

happening. The museum staff gathered around. We all laughed at the sweet scene. Thomas opened the cage and put his finger up to Pai; she jumped on. He brought her to his face and they played "nosey"—something they often had done. Meanwhile, Tweeter happily flew out and circled the room, singing. The reunion was enchanting and joyous. Before we left, Thomas spoke to the birds, giving them his gentlest good-bye.

That night, Thomas dressed in his favorite billowy white cotton shirt, jeans, and boots. His parents drove us to the concert hall. The show had begun, and we were brought to the wing of the stage where we watched the various bands perform and saw the audience. His parents and brother sat in the hall near the front. The auditorium was filled, with standing room only. We were touched by all of the wonderful music and heartfelt tributes. Meanwhile, rumors spread through the hall that Thomas might play. No one knew for sure, least of all myself. Then during intermission, Thomas—moved by all of the music and love he felt— said to his band members, "I want to play."

When the second half of the program started, they called Thomas to the microphone. As he slowly walked across the stage, the audience stood and applauded; many had tears in their eyes. Thomas, too. Most had not seen Thomas for more than a year. He thanked everyone for their support and expressed his love. "I probably have breath for only ten minutes of good sound," he half-joked to the audience. Then he raised the flute to his lips; he played for a full twenty minutes.

That giant spirit, which he had always been on-stage, came to life. With overwhelming power, Thomas played the most exquisite ballad, each note clear and articulated, a melody haunting and soaring. The tune was a favorite he had composed called "Aeolus" (God of the Wind). When it was over, everyone stood, breathless, clapping and crying. Thomas looked out as if he were memorizing every single face that was in the hall. Then he smiled, put his hands to his heart, and took a bow.

At his parents' house, Thomas, while uplifted by the evening, was exhausted. It was late, but after a warm bath, he slept comfortably. In the morning, he awoke with a fever, and the next day he was admitted to the hospital. It was pneumonia. We both knew this was the end. "I'm at peace," he told me, "because of Sunday." He meant the night of the concert when he had played one last time. We said what were to be our last "I love you's." Then Thomas was placed in intensive care and ten days later he passed on. He died doing what he loved and fulfilling his deepest wish to play: not because I want to play, because I must.

Nine months after Thomas had died, the building super came to the apartment to fix a bathroom pipe. He spoke of Thomas and how much he had liked him. He had seen Thomas perform once, he said, and had enjoyed it very much. As he was leaving, he paused in the doorway. "By the way, do you remember Moi, the kitten that lived in the basement?" he asked. "Well, right after Thomas died, she just disappeared."

Some days I imagine Thomas, over there, playing some raucous jazz, with Moi turning somersaults at his feet. Thomas is laughing, doing what he loves.

Peace for Pickles

B. J. Taylor

There she was one day, looking sad-eyed and mournful, peering in through the glass patio door. Her silky fur was jet black and her eyes were as big as saucers. As I gazed at her I spoke the thought that was running through my head, "My, you are in quite a pickle."

This beautiful, regal cat was definitely pregnant. Her stomach was bulging, and she appeared ready to give birth any day. I gathered a blanket, a basket, and a bowl of milk, and I opened the patio door. I walked outside, and she backed up about ten feet, watching with wary eyes as I set down the bowl and arranged the blanket in the basket.

"It's okay, sweetheart," I said softly. "Here's some milk and a fluffy blanket to lie on. You're such a pretty kitty. Do you have a home? Does anyone take care of you?"

I went back inside the house, wondering where she had come from. I had seen a black cat in our neighborhood but assumed she was someone's pet.

"That cat has been around for years," a neighbor said a few days later. "She's had at least fifteen litters of kittens."

"Has anyone tried to take her to the vet for spaying?" I asked.

"Some of us have tried to catch her, but she's smart and gets away every time."

I had already asked myself why this homeless black beauty came to my door. She looked as sad as I felt. Losing my father after a long illness, my days and nights were no longer filled with phone calls and visits. I felt frustrated, alone, and weary. I couldn't even muster up my faith. Everything looked bleak.

Remembering my dad's caring ways was the only comfort I had right now. He loved animals and had a soft spot in his heart for every stray. When I was a little girl, our house was a revolving door for abandoned cats and dogs brought home by my dad after finding them in the restrooms of the gas station he owned. He would have wanted me to take care of this one.

So eventually as I sat drinking a cup of coffee one morning, I watched this beautiful cat through the glass door. "Okay, Dad, I'm going to keep her," I spoke aloud. "She needs a home."

What are you going to call her? I could almost hear him say. "I'm going to name her Pickles."

She must have had a hard life surviving on her own all those years. I had a strong feeling it was time now to give her a break. *Just like it was time for Dad to get a break.* After all his years of struggling with his illness, it was his time for some peace. I knew that in my heart but had trouble with it in my head.

I decided that after Pickles' babies were born, I'd get her spayed so she could live out the rest of her life in peace. It would be something I could focus on during the lonely days and weeks ahead. I didn't realize it would be much harder than I thought to make my promise to Pickles come true.

Over the next few days, Pickles came to drink the milk and eat the food I put out for her, but would then disappear. One morning, I saw a tiny black kitten curled up in the blanket-lined basket outside the back door. Then I looked up.

There in the street was Pickles, running right in front of a car. The brakes squealed and the driver slowed, and fortunately Pickles survived a near miss. . . . I could see her carrying a solid gray kitten by the nape of its neck. Bouncing across the yard, she deposited it in the basket and took off again. She made three more trips for a total of five kittens.

the cat slinks, it slank,
it has slunk around the house
a lesson in verbs

Cautiously, I made my way around the side of the house to get a closer look at the new babies. I longed to hold Pickles and snuggle her close, but her years of living in the wild made her wary of human contact. Without knowing it, though, she was helping me to keep my mind off my own problems. I peered into the basket and watched as she licked and cleaned the kittens, wishing I could pet each one, but holding back until the time was right.

Over the next few weeks, Pickles proved to be an excellent mother. Even though she looked exhausted, she spent hours feeding, cleaning, and tending to her babies. As they grew, she watched them eat the food that was put out for them, never taking a bite herself until all of the kittens were through.

Over time, I felt my own weariness lifting. I sure didn't feel alone when I came home to six pairs of hungry eyes watching me through the patio door. I even started to laugh again, and surprised myself with the sweet, familiar sound. It was such fun watching the kittens roll around on top of each other and play hide-and-seek under the edges of the blanket.

Whenever Pickles would let me, I'd sit down next to the basket and pet each kitten in turn. As I stroked each furry little ball, I soothingly crooned, "It's okay, Pickles. I won't hurt them. They're so cute with big eyes like yours and soft fur. Look at this one with the black-and-white mask on her face. She looks like a little bandit. And this solid black one looks just like you."

Grow Your Own

Plant your own catnip garden. You can buy catnip as a plant or as seeds; it's usually called catmint in your garden or feed store and can be found in the herb section. Catnip is very hardy and needs no particular care, and once you get a patch started, you'll have plenty. Catnip is in the mint family, and mint spreads like a weed, so don't plant this in your flower garden. At harvesttime, pick and place in a big bucket to dry. When drying is done, stuff plants and their seeds into an old sock, and watch your cat get happy. And probably all the other cats in the neighborhood, too.

Pickles seemed to understand my contact with the kittens was necessary, and it sure did my heart good. Sometimes, though, the sad tears would flow as I thought of how much I missed my dad. Then Pickles would look at me with those big eyes that seemed to say, *Everything's going to be all right. You take care of me and I'll take care of you.* Did she know how much I needed her?

When the kittens were old enough, I found homes for four of the five. The antics of every kitten endeared me to each one, but the solid gray one stood out among the rest. He was soft and cuddly. When he stood up and stretched his paws against the door he looked just like a bear, so that's what I called him.

It was time now to make good on my promise. I needed to take Pickles to be spayed before she became pregnant again. I thought it would be easy to put her in a cat carrier and take her to the vet. Boy, was I wrong.

The first attempt failed miserably. I placed a small bowl of food inside a plastic carrier and set it outside. Pickles stood back about thirty feet with her nose in the air and glared at the carrier. "Come on, sweetie, go in and eat a little bit," I tried, coaxing her to step in. She wouldn't even go near it.

For the second attempt, I ran a string from the carrier's door into the house. *Maybe if she didn't see me, she'd go inside*, I thought. My plan was to close the hinged door by pulling on the string. I used a little tuna on a plate for bait, and this time she went all the way in. I pulled the string, the door almost shut, and she went berserk, bolting through the carrier's plastic door.

"Oh, Pickles, I'm not trying to hurt you," I tried to reassure her in a soothing voice. "We both know you have to go to the vet. Please, just walk inside."

With her enormous size and strength, I should have known a plastic carrier was not going to work. After running off about twenty feet, she turned around and looked back at me as if to say, "You tricked me. I don't like being caged."

Unsure of what to do next, I took my plea to a higher power. "God, I need your help," I whispered. "I promised Pickles I'd help her find peace. Would you help me?"

Later that day I felt myself being guided to the phone. Once there, I called the vet's office. After I explained my dilemma, they said they had a metal cage I could borrow, which had a trap door used most often to catch wild animals that needed medical care. It sounded like the perfect answer.

I carried the cage to the backyard and talked to Pickles, who sat in the corner watching me. "Look at this one, Pickles. It's much bigger and you can see through it. When you go inside, the door will shut behind you, but don't be afraid."

At the vet's suggestion, I placed a piece of chicken in the corner of the cage, with the metal door propped open on its spring-loaded hinge. All Pickles had to do was approach the bait. What happened next seemed like a miracle. With a slow, calm, steady gait, Pickles walked straight into the cage, almost as if a loving hand was guiding her. No backward glance, no hesitation, and no thrashing or trying to escape. Her weight pressed down on the spring and the door shut behind her.

She sat inside the cage, a calm surrounding her. She didn't struggle at all.

I began to marvel at her acceptance and surrender. *Is that what it takes?* I wondered. *Acceptance? Maybe that's what's lacking in my own life.*

The vet operated that day, and when I picked Pickles up she was sporting a shaved stomach and dissolvable stitches. She was groggy from the anesthesia so I was advised to leave her in the cage overnight. The next morning Pickles awoke and peered at me with those big saucer eyes. I let her out of the cage at the side of the house; she took a few steps, then turned and looked at me. Our eyes locked and I saw my own newfound serenity reflected in hers.

A few months later I took Bear in to be neutered. Now mother and son live with me. Each morning and evening when I feed them, Bear rubs against my legs, and Pickles will sometimes allow me one small pat on the top of her head, befitting her aloof stature as queen of the yard.

The gentle, guiding hand that showed Pickles the way to peace also showed me the way to acceptance and contentment. I found out that when you help others, you forget all about your own troubles. With her son at her side, Pickles now has a life of leisure. They play in the bushes, chase each other up trees, and lie in the sun on warm days. I'm happy to say that Pickles is no longer homeless, and I am no longer lonely.

Empty Arms

Linda Shands

Our youngest grandchild had just turned three, the last of our cats had gone, and our twin golden retrievers had reached middle age. I needed someone to cuddle, but my arms were empty.

"Time for another cat!" I announced to my reluctant spouse.

He rolled his eyes. "Fine, as long as you take care of it."

A short time later, I claimed a kitten from a friend. The mama cat was famous for sweet-tempered, beautiful babies. But instead of a plump, round ball of fur, I cradled in the palm of one hand a scrawny little animal, all tail and ears.

"Her name is Molly," my friend told me. "We think the others were pushing her away from the food." The kitten blinked up at me and began a rumbling purr.

"Don't worry, little one," I crooned as I carried her out to the SUV, "we'll get you fattened up in no time."

I placed her in a basket in the back of the car and hurried to the front. There she sat, smack in the middle of the driver's seat. "You are fast," I chuckled, "but I can't have you getting under my feet." I took her back to the basket and set a book on the lid. Just as I started the engine, I felt the sting of tiny claws dig into my shoulder as a moist little nose prodded my ear.

Wonderful, I thought, *I've adopted a feline Houdini!* I let the car roll backwards out of the parking space. Instead of bolting, Molly tucked herself into the hollow between my neck and shoulder and sat, alert as any co-pilot, for the entire forty-mile drive home.

In no time this tiny tyrant had the household under her control. She raced from room to room, investigated every possible hiding place, selected various nap accommodations, and had both ninety-pound golden retrievers trembling in their fur. She claimed squatter rights on the dog's water bowl and nibbled at her food but was easily distracted and not inclined to eat a meal.

In spite of her feisty personality, she preferred human transportation to her own paws. "You're a little pest," I chided as she begged for attention. But when she learned to crawl up my pant leg and scramble into my arms, I realized it was easier on my clothes, not to mention my skin, to just pick her up. My maternal instinct kicked in and I automatically rocked her as I would a baby. Her satisfied purr was ample reward.

Our mutual contentment was short-lived as Molly began to reject all but a few bites of food. I held her through the night while she vomited and meowed in pain. Tears soaked my sweatshirt as I cradled her in my arms. She was little more than a pile of fur-covered bones, yet she still purred and licked the tears off my chin.

"Oh, God," I begged throughout that endless night, "she has filled a hole in my life; please don't take her away."

The moment the sun swept light into the eastern sky, I tucked my new fur baby inside my sweatshirt and headed for the vet clinic. As I carefully maneuvered the car into town, I felt her little body tremble next to my heart. Thankful that I'd known this doctor for many years, I carried Molly gently into his office. She meowed pitifully as a vet assistant whisked her away.

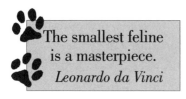

The smallest feline is a masterpiece.
Leonardo da Vinci

A few minutes later the doctor returned alone. "The X-rays show a blockage in Molly's intestine," he said. "If we're going to operate it has to be now."

Doctor Bill sat on the edge of the exam table waiting for my answer. "I'd say her chances of making it through surgery are fifty-fifty." He prodded gently, "Not great odds, but not impossible."

"She's yours," my husband had said. "You take care of her."

Molly had been with me less than a week. Could I justify spending money that would involve a sacrifice for our family on a ten-week-old kitten with only a 50 percent chance for life?

"We have to try," I told Doctor Bill. He patted my shoulder, then disappeared into the surgery room.

I watched the clock and prayed. In the few short days I'd known her, Molly had become as dear to me as a baby. Now I might lose her. I was reminded how God cares for the birds of the air and clothes the flowers of the field. Molly was in good hands.

Hours later, the vet finally called me at home. "Molly made it through surgery, but we're not out of the woods." He went on to explain that they had removed four inches of bowel from this tiny animal. Then he told me, "I'm taking her home with me so I can keep an eye on her."

When I arrived at the clinic the next morning, I found all three veterinarians and most of the staff supervising the patient. "I would never have believed it." The doctor's assistant grinned. "If we can get her to eat, I'd say her chances are about 75 percent."

Molly hobbled around the floor on spindly legs encumbered by a huge splint that still held the catheter needle. When she saw me, she meowed frantically, sprinted across the room, and jumped into my arms. Her rumbling purr all but drowned out the laughter as her amazed caretakers shook their heads.

An aide brought in a bowl of cat milk and a can of recovery-diet food. Molly licked the mixture off my finger then lapped up half of the meager meal. The three doctors looked at each other. "Take her home," they agreed. "She's better off with you."

To keep her warm and content, I fashioned my sweatshirt into a sling and carried her everywhere. As she improved, she graduated from her fleece cocoon to my shoulder, where she watched me work.

Several weeks of round-the-clock nursing, hand feeding, and generally trying to keep up with a kitten that did not know she was an invalid left me exhausted. But a tiny black nose pressed against mine, a rumbling purr when I said her name, or a toy mouse dropped at my feet caused me to lift a prayer of gratitude to God for the gift of Molly's life.

Now full grown, Molly is long and slender with tufted ears, piercing emerald eyes, silk-soft fur, and an enormous puffy tail. She still won't finish a meal unless I feed her, but she can dispatch a real mouse with one swift nip. She races across the fields, leaving both dogs in the dust.

She doesn't seem to notice that she no longer fits in the palm of one hand. Now when she jumps up to cuddle, she amply fills both empty arms.

Out of the Woods

Jeanette Thomason

The first winter I lived in a house on the rim of Central Oregon's Cascades, I woke before dawn one morning to see a little cat running through the woods along the top of a deep, crusted snow. In the last moonlight's gleam I watched the cat, a little thing, trot along the tree line, tail straight in the air, like she was late for some important date.

I never saw her face and couldn't make out her color, just her shape. It was early and I was cold, not quite awake. I rubbed the sleep from my eyes to get a better look. But when I peered out the window again, there was no cat, just the shine of untracked snow.

The fire had died, and my feet slapped the tiles down a long hallway to the kitchen. I arranged kindling over last night's ashes and reached under the window bin for wood. Pulling up two logs, I looked outside again. The sun hadn't fully risen and the Ponderosa pines lining the edge of the yard cast pointy shadows through the gray of a lifting night. The icy crust, formed over several feet of snow, stretched into the trees. Come spring I would discover that underneath all that snow there was a picnic table. I'd moved here in the dead of winter, the deep of it when snow, snow, and then more snow had piled up. So much snow had fallen, the world out my back window seemed a step higher to the mountains—the trees shorter, the fading stars somehow closer, within reach, and the heavens more real than the horizon beneath.

I stood transfixed by the sky before the last glints of the falling moonlight made me shiver and I started the fire, then the coffee. I returned to the window with a steaming mug.

Sometimes, before dawn, if I was still enough, patient enough, mule deer would slip into the backyard and linger. I waited, hopeful. The steam began to glaze my view so I smeared the window clear with a pajama sleeve. I studied the mountains: majestic Mount Jefferson on the right, each of its slopes like a profile of Bob Hope's nose. To its left, Three Fingered Jack, a craggy peak shaped like a fist raising its pointer finger and thumb; then Black Butte, and parentheses-shaped Mount Washington, and the Three Sisters—known to the first settlers here as Faith, Hope, and Charity.

But something on the ground between the mountain edge and the forest caught my attention.

The cat.

She looked at me. Into me. Then she beelined for the door, tail straight in the air.

There was no mistake. I was the important date for which she was late.

I set down my mug and moved for the door, then the deck, at the same time as the little cat. What would a cat be doing in the woods in below-freezing temperatures? Was she lost? Had she been dumped? But who would drive so far to dump a little cat? I was living on the edge of U.S. Forest Service land; my backyard was Ponderosa pines up to the edge of the Cascade foothills.

Surprisingly, when I stepped into the dimly silent morning, the little cat didn't hesitate, just trotted up the deck. Her demeanor spoke: How do you do? Fine morning to you. She stood six feet from me, looking up into my face. I could feel, not just see her regarding me as I studied her funny shape: stocky chest, short front legs, short-haired white form with downy calico brown and gray tabby spots. Patchwork coat. Dainty feet and face. Andy Rooney eyebrows. She was a funny-looking thing. Petite, and yet hearty, right at home in these woods. A cat who had been around the block, all hood, all-knowing, all street. Gangsta cat, but with a little Grace Kelly underneath.

black-rimmed, almond eyes
oh to be as beautiful
as the calico

151

Smitten, I could only stare.

She stepped right up and spoke first: meow.

Her meow was direct, plain, clear. Not a tentative whisper, not a question, not a plea. A hello. A here I am, there you are.

"Well, hello, little cat."

Everyone, cat lover or not, knows this rule: feed a stray and it will stay.

Why not? Free lunch. Free lodging. Plain affection. Good enough.

The thing is, on our first meeting no food was offered, no promise to come inside, no encouraging greeting or display of affection from me. Just a face-to-face. Simply some presence.

But the cat had regarded me, and I the cat, and there was no doubt. This was a cat to sit with on a fallen log and drink a cuppa joe and watch the sunrise, to walk through woods side-by-side, to watch birds together, to collect pinecones (me) and bugs (the cat) from the yard. This was a cat that didn't need coddling; I was a person with no urge to domesticate or anthropomorphize, no need to take pictures of kitty for my desk at work, no desire for little cubic zirconia collars or jackets. Plain Cat. Plain Girl. We were taken with each other.

So out came the food, which the cat gladly accepted.

I trudged to the woodshed to look for a couple of spare boxes that could be transformed into a kitty igloo with a few old rugs and towels, and an old blanket destined for Goodwill anyway. Within a day, a box on the deck became a bed in the kitchen; a place to stay for a night or two became indefinite digs in the corner.

It was all temporary, of course. I was already making "Found" signs to put up at the post office and our only grocery store in town. Besides, I already had a cat who owned the place: Miss Kitty, who, like her Gunsmoke namesake, was no nonsense and sometimes all spit to exercise her run of the place.

Miss Kitty, a small and long-haired tabby, had made my home hers four years previous. She came to me like a library book checked in and out, nerves shot and pupils dilated, through a friend who believed in rescuing felines, from a neighbor's house that was ruled by dogs with a taste for cat tail, three squirrelly elementary-age kids, and a part-time day-care business.

Glad for the quiet and open range of a single girl's home, Kitty quickly took ownership of the place on her own terms. She eased out of her traumatic beginnings by spending the first week hiding out in the bathroom drawer, accessed from cabinet doors she learned to open in the House of Dog Horrors, and nesting well out of sight of ghosts of creatures past on top of a couple combs and hairbrushes. The second week she moved to quarters under the bed; by week three she'd taken up residence in the sliver of space between the top of the refrigerator and the cabinets above.

Week four she emerged a new creature to run the place with strict rules and a serious sense of territory: She would sit not on your lap but beside you. She didn't need to be picked up or held. If she wanted your company she'd take it, but not before or without her permission, and when she was done, she was *done*. The green leather chair was hers. She didn't take calls like a dog and would not be ordered like a steak.

In her own time, never when called, she would down the occasional shot of milk. You could scratch the top of her head behind the ears but never touch the tail. If she was happy, she might half-drool, half-purr, but even asleep, she would always keep a green eye on you from beneath a heavy fringe of black lashes so long they looked fake. She was Miss Kitty, all right, minus the blue eye shadow and petticoat, content to take or leave any Matt Dillon and, to some degree, in a completely feline fine way, me.

I was the litter service, after all. The chef. The Help.

So when Miss Kitty saw The Help pour kibble into her bowl . . . and then a second, heaping one that was trotted out the back door, she suspected something was terribly, horribly wrong.

Once uninterested in my comings and goings to the back deck, Miss Kitty became obsessed with Outside. Where was the extra bowl of kibble going? What's going on out there anyway? She began to hover near that door; her already pom-pom–like hair electrified into an angrier and angrier bouffant.

To Be or Not to Be . . . Outdoors

Many of us were raised to believe cats should be allowed the run of the outdoors. But we do live in a fallen world, and the fact is, cats who roam live shorter lives than cats who don't roam. Dangers from both man and beast are out there, and so are virulent cat diseases, transmitted from cat to cat. You can add an average of ten years to your cat's life if you keep her indoors. An indoor cat can be very happy as long as there are: windows providing sunlight, activities to watch, things to climb, space to chase (preferably in circles), clean litter, and daily interaction with someone who plays.[6]

As I got acquainted outside with New Cat, I could see Miss Kitty, face and front paws pressed against the door window. She had climbed on top of the washer in the back kitchen corner and was straddled, straining precariously, between appliance and window. (Good thing, no petticoat.)

And she was ticked.

Miss Kitty was backed in a corner, no gun, no Festus, nothing to do but channel Stanley from Tennessee Williams's *Streetcar Named Desire*, only Stanley in reverse, inside, looking out.

Her claws sprang from spread paws to ping the glass.

Stel-la. Stellll-aaahhhhh. . . .

The name stuck. So did Miss Kitty, glued there to the window, back feet in a perfect Barbie shoe, tiptoe arch on the washer top. This routine went on for a couple days in which Stella seemed unfazed by the frantic window press behind me every time I came onto the deck. She stared blankly at Kitty, then turned to the food, all cool, ever mellow and matter-of-fact, which Kitty took as invitation to a showdown.

Later that week, when temperatures dropped and snow flurries began again, I invited Stella inside. I parked her little cardboard igloo bed in the corner of the kitchen by the woodstove, which had never interested Miss Kitty before. But then before, Kitty had the run of the place; now she wasn't so sure. All she knew was she'd had her fill of days living not so sure. She'd reached her limit.

Miss Kitty sputtered into an angry ball and sat hunched at the edge of the kitchen, blocking entrance to the living room and the green Queen Anne chair, cutting off access down the hallway that led to the bedrooms. No way was Stella going crossing into the private sanctum. No way was The Help telling her how things were going to be.

Good enough, Stella seemed to say. She was, of course, Gangsta cat. She probably could have taken Miss Kitty faster than cook Paula Dean could say "butter," but why risk getting kicked out of the new digs? She, matter-of-fact, just like that trot from the woods, began to groom herself; then she sidled up to the woodstove and curled into a ball, tail tucked under calloused paws, for a long winter's nap.

The indifference (or was it lack of fear?) infuriated Miss Kitty, who began to plot a showdown. (Never mind that Stella preferred outside to in by day and seemed to want in only on the cold nights.)

After a few nights of midnight cat screams and scuffles, I decided it wasn't fair for Stella or Miss Kitty to have to tolerate one another any longer. Someone was going to have to get out of Dodge.

At the women's magazine where I worked, we had a new art director who became a fast friend. Laurie had just moved to our small mountain town from Seattle, and she'd rented a house eight miles east of town, in even deeper woods where homes were interspersed miles apart and then tucked out of sight into the trees. Even living in the more populated area six miles west of town, I knew what Laurie meant when she said she loathed driving home through the pines that blocked even the moonlight, going home to an empty house, knocking around in the silence.

She needed a pet.

Cats are great, I confided. Perfect companions. Every cat lover knows the feline virtues. A cat doesn't have to be entertained or fussed over. Cats can make play with simple things: string, a leaky faucet, toilet paper. A cat cleans up after itself. Cats will always listen, always consider with wise eyes what you have to say. Cats talk back too, but not all chattery like a bird, or breathlessly and needy for response like a dog. Some cats mew a "welcome home" when you walk in the door. Others talk with the flick of a tail

A cat is more intelligent than people believe, and can be taught any crime.

Mark Twain

raised up and at the tip curling into a question mark, or with a gentle nudge of the head to your leg. But there's no barking, no begging to mess with, no taking over half the bed or stinking like dirty socks after a walk in the rain.

Laurie began to imagine the comforts and joys of a cat—coming home to the promise of a good book, a toasty fire, and a companion that would never track muddy footprints across the floor and always purr when scratched under the chin.

Perfect, we agreed.

Laurie would come by my house Saturday to meet Stella.

The meeting went well.

Laurie loved Stella's unafraid, pointer walk straight to her; Stella liked the way Laurie didn't try to coddle her, just scratched her on the head, plain and straightforward-like. A handshake. A done deal. Happy campers, all.

And so that was that. I scooped up Stella and gave her a kiss on the head. Stella didn't resist. Just smiled her petite calico cat smile. I felt her heart beat stronger through that stocky, thick chest. Even gangstas need love.

We walked to Laurie's car and Laurie reached for her new companion. Stella seemed eager and hopped onto the front seat, where she sat, unaffected, still, cool. She was like that, Stella, ever present, ever ready for what came her way. Today, an afternoon drive through the woods? Fine.

But as Laurie shut the door, started the engine, and pulled away, I saw the flash in Stella's eyes. Not panic. Not fear. Just a question. Coming?

I stood in the snow and watched the car head down the drive. Towering Ponderosas shielded what little afternoon sun broke through clouds heavy with the promise of more snow. I suddenly felt the weight in those clouds. How could I have become so attached in just a week to that little cat? She never slept on my bed, but was affectionate and loved crawling onto my lap and feeling the weight of a hardcover book resting on her back, or—when Miss Kitty staked this territory that had never interested her before—just being in the same room. Stella followed me, in fact, through and out of the house. Always eager for a scratch or hoist up and cuddles under my chin, but just as happy across the room by the woodstove or at my feet, or walking alongside me as I piled up wood to bring inside for drying out. Just face-to-face time mattered. Presence.

As the car headed into the distance, I saw Stella's funny-shaped, petite frame—stocky chest, short legs—perched between the front seats. I couldn't make out her face, just her silhouette, but I knew she was looking straight at me.

Meow.

Here I am.

There you are.

Behind me, Miss Kitty, green eyes wide, craned her fluffy neck from her stance on a chair, paws pressed in relief against the front room window glass.

The next Monday, I checked in with Laurie. How's Stella doing? How are you two getting along?

What a cutie, Laurie gushed. Stella seemed to groove in her new home—and Laurie was as well, she said. She didn't dread going home so much; she talked more about the great books she was reading by a roaring fire with her little friend. Stella entertained Laurie by walking along the railing of the loft over the living room, chattering at birds outside the wall of windows to the deck, rolling pinecones from the basket by the fireplace and across the floor.

I was eager for more detail, but Laurie was a big-picture girl.

At dinner several weeks later with Laurie and another colleague and mutual friend, I asked for more news. "Stella all settled in?"

"Oh yeah," Laurie said, her voice slightly higher than normal. She grabbed the menu with one hand and waved over our waiter with the other. "Hey, anyone want some hors d'oeuvres?"

"Yeah, that Stella," I nudged—

"The artichoke dip is fabulous," Laurie said, imitating Scooby Doo's Scooby snack noise.

"Ooh, artichoke dip," Kathy chimed in.

The waiter stood at my corner of the table, pen poised as I scanned the menu. "Yep, that Stella's a keeper . . ."

Apparently, though, Stella was not. After dinner, as Laurie and Kathy and I separated to our cars, Kathy pulled me aside. We waved good-bye to Laurie, already at her car and hopping in to start the engine.

"You didn't hear it from me," Kathy said out of the side of her mouth, head turned, "but Laurie hasn't seen that cat in a week."

What? "What do you mean?"

Kathy looked side to side, like one of those fearful wives on *The Sopranos*. "The cat kept wanting out and last Monday made a run for it when Laurie opened the door to go to work." Kathy nodded good-bye, smiling plastic-like to Laurie driving out of the lot. "She's been looking through the woods for a week and can't find sign of hide nor hair."

"But why—" I started to ask the obvious.

"Laurie didn't want you to know, 'cause she's afraid that cat's been food for wolves."

I raised my brows in lament.

"Sorry," Kathy responded, turning to her car, "but you know these woods. Laurie feels awful, just terrible. She can't even talk about it."

I knew these woods. I drove home through them, through sentinels of dark, towering pines in silence. If there was one thing I could count on like mule deer in the backyard on still mornings, it was the yip yip yip of coyotes at midnight on dark quiet mountain nights.

I couldn't help the tears as I unlocked the door and found Miss Kitty waiting, for once, wanting to be picked up and held. She purred as I cuddled her head under my neck, newfound appreciation, thanks to Stella's example.

Kitty never knew the comfort she offered on behalf of her worst enemy and my little friend—the sort of friend that even though you haven't seen her in a while leaves a vacant hole in your heart when irrevocably gone.

Though we never talked of Stella again, Laurie must have wondered why I stopped asking about her. When we each relocated soon after to different states, Laurie and I drifted into the kind of friendship that's remained strong (for more than fifteen years now) based on shared work and sensibilities and creative endeavors. But there are some things, among even friends, you just don't talk about, and we maintained an unspoken, mysterious agreement that the topic of Stella would be ours.

Our mutual friend and colleague, Kathy, understood this. She swears, over all these years, she never told Laurie about betraying the confidence of Stella's escape, not even the part about how the week after such revelation I drove home late from work on the magazines one night to see an odd shadow that seemed to race beside my car down my long treed drive.

The night was especially black, though a sliver of early moonlight tried valiantly to bounce off the mounds of compact snow covering the drive and forest floor. I'd rubbed my eyes, thinking my weariness was playing tricks on me. No wild creature would run alongside a car. But the silhouette in the headlights was unmistakable.

Petite frame. Short legs. Stocky little chest. And tail straight in the air.

I parked under the pine by the front deck and stepped out of the car. Stella made a beeline for me, weary, grimy, calloused paws padding over still-crusted snow.

I scooped her up, squeezing her funny little frame to me, rubbing her calico cat smile against my cheek, knowing we would find a way for peace to come to Dodge. We would find a way for presence with Miss Kitty inside the house, and face-to-face time with Stella outside. Love finds a way, even across the miles, even through the dark.

This time I was quick to speak first.

"Welcome home, little cat."

An April Fool's Prayer

Bonnie Compton Hanson

M om! Mom!"
In blew three small, bundled-up boys and a crisp October wind.

"Mom! There's a cat down in the ground!"

I looked up blankly from the stove. "Uh—you mean someone's cat died?"

"No, Mom! Please! Come see! She needs help!"

Six eager hands pulled me outside and down to the curb in front of our house. Five-year-old Robin pointed. "Listen! Can't you hear her?"

Yes, I could—a very faint meow. Floating right up from the storm drain.

"We've got to get her out!" he cried.

Chat, almost four, squinted down into the darkness. "Maybe we could drop her a rope."

Two-and-a-half-year-old Jay started calling, "Hey, kitty, kitty, kitty!"

By now a crowd of neighborhood children had gathered around. "This storm sewer drains into the peat bog across the street," one of the older boys explained. "If we go down there and call, maybe she'll come out."

"Well, all right," I agreed. "But everyone's got to stay right with me."

Beyond the edge of the developed lots we found the culvert opening. Water barely trickled out of it, headed down to a large swamp. But a big storm was forecast for that very night. If we didn't rescue the cat now, it would probably drown.

"Kitty! Kitty!" the children all shouted at once.

"Shh!" I protested. "You'll scare her away. Let's take turns instead."

So one by one they called. Jay was last. "Here, kitty, kitty, kitty!"

Finally out she came. Muddy, wet, painfully thin, with a woefully deformed tail. But alive.

"Whose cat is she?" I asked.

"No one's," piped up one of the girls. "Her old owners kicked her down there."

"Well, she's ours now," Robin announced. "'Cause Jay's the one she came out for."

Back at the house, we wiped the pathetic creature off the best we could. Then I filled a bowl of milk for her.

But ignoring the milk completely, she sat and washed herself all over. Now we could see that she was a longhair with striking black-and-white markings. Only when she was immaculate did she turn to the dish. Even then, instead of gulping it down, she sipped daintily, stopping to clean her whiskers from time to time.

"Look at that!" my husband, Don, exclaimed. "She's a real lady."

And that's how Ladycat came to be with us.

Just in time, too. For all night long, fierce north-westerlies roared across the prairie, with wave after wave of pounding rain that quickly changed to snow.

But inside, our home glowed with the joy of a new playmate. For hours on end, Ladycat would play ball, blocks, and car with three enchanted boys. At Christmastime, watching her delight in gift wrappings and ornaments was almost more fun than presents.

Ladycat blossomed under this love. Her long silky hair, love for fun, and sweet ways quickly won everyone over. Only two things about her past remained: her deformed tail (perhaps broken in that kick down the storm drain), and her need to go outside and hunt for at least an hour every night.

Frozen days rolled into frozen weeks of ten, twenty, thirty degrees below zero. By the middle of February, cabin fever was getting to us all.

Then for Valentine's Day all three boys got a present: chicken pox—Chat so severely, he went into a coma and had to be hospitalized. His brothers begged me not to let Ladycat out that night, in case something would happen to her as well.

But the air that evening had turned balmy—almost springlike—with just a little drizzle. "Don't worry, she'll be right back," I assured them.

Quickly, though, that drizzle whipped itself up into a wild rainstorm. And for the very first time, Ladycat did not come back. All night long, as I cared for Jay and Robin, I kept listening for her discreet call. But I heard only the rain. Until the rain stopped and everything froze.

The next morning Don's car slipped and slid all over the ice-covered road as he drove the long miles to work. But he couldn't call me to let me know he got there okay. I couldn't even call the hospital fifteen miles away to check on Chat. Or turn on the radio. Or lights. Or heater.

Because under the weight of that ice, the power and phone lines had snapped. Even our gas-powered furnace and water heater were inoperable, since they were triggered electrically.

Washer, refrigerator—equally useless. Nothing worked but our gas stove.

By the time Don reached home that night, he was coughing badly. But at least his office had been warm. At home, the boys had to be bundled up in their snow-suits all day long—complete misery with all those itching pox! By evening, both boys also had bronchitis.

But sick as they were, they kept going to the living room window, looking and calling for their missing pet.

Late that night, Don woke up in excruciating pain with a grossly swollen abdomen. And even though it was well below freezing outside and freezing inside, his whole body was afire.

Searching my first aid book by candlelight, I gasped. "Don, I think you have appendicitis."

All the usual procedures at that point—calling 911 or the doctor or an ambulance—went by the boards. We couldn't even reach our nearest neighbor. And I didn't dare leave Robin and Jay home alone to take Don to the hospital—or take them out into the bitter cold, sick as they were.

I've Been to the Desert . . .

Cats are originally desert creatures. Why else would they like that hot sunlight directly on their fur? They do not require a lot of water, especially if they eat canned food. An unfortunate part of this desert legacy, however, is that when Mr. Cat is ailing, he will often stop drinking. In a couple of days, some real damage can happen. One way to know if you have a sick cat is to take a bowl of clean water to him and see if he'll drink. It's also a considerate thing to do when your cat has a cold.

Don would have to go alone.

As quickly as possible, I packed ice around his abdomen, covered that with towels, threw a winter coat over his pajamas, and sent him out into the night, praying he'd be able to make it to the hospital without passing out. Or ending up in a wreck.

By the next day Robin, Jay, and I all had pneumonia. But so did almost everyone else in our heatless suburb. Indeed, with so many sick, only the most critically ill could be admitted to the hospital. I learned later that Don had to sit up in a waiting room all that night—with ruptured appendix, peritonitis, and double pneumonia—before they could even find a bed for him.

Finally, after a week, power and phones returned. After two weeks, so did Don, for a long convalescence.

And after three weeks, Chat did, too. But not our missing cat.

February blurred into March, one storm following another. The same with illnesses: measles, German measles, several strep infections. Finally Chat came down with rheumatic fever—in such pain he couldn't be touched without screaming.

"It's all because Ladycat left," Robin sobbed one day. "Why doesn't she come back? Doesn't she love us anymore? Doesn't God love us anymore?"

I fought tears at that, because in my despair I asked the very same question. *Dear God, why are you letting this happen to these innocent children? Don't you love us anymore?*

"Well, God knows where Ladycat is," Chat replied weakly. "And I'm going to pray and ask him to bring her back home to us. In time for Jay's birthday!"

Jay's third birthday, on April second, was just a few days away. What an impossible prayer!

Though the last day of March was as white, cold, and dreary as ever, on April first the wind shifted. And the skies opened up.

"Look, children!" I cried. "It's raining cats and dogs!"

All three rushed to the living room window. "Cats!" Jay cried. "Is Ladycat back?"

"She will be," Chat assured him. "For your birthday."

Oh, what a cruel April Fool's joke—to have such impossible faith!

Changing the subject, I asked, "What do you want for your birthday, Jay?"

Nose pressed against the glass: "Ladycat. Just Ladycat."

That evening the rain finally let up. Then at the dinner table, Robin suddenly put down his fork. "What's that noise?"

"The wind, dear," I replied.

"No, someone's at the front door. Who is it?"

"Ladycat!" Jay shouted. All three boys ran to the front door, flinging it open wide.

A biting wind roared in—followed by a tiny, mud-covered creature, barely able to move.

Don jumped up. "Quick! Get her some food!"

But as feeble as she was, the cat slowly, painfully cleaned herself all over. Only then would she eat. Ladycat was back.

The next morning we retraced her tiny footsteps in the mud—all the way to the culvert where we had first found her. Ever since the ice storm—that night she had disappeared—the opening had been completely frozen over. Until yesterday's warm April Fool's rain.

What an April Fool *I* had been! For that frozen-over opening had melted just in time for Jay's birthday. Just in time to answer an April Fool's prayer, helping one little cat and three little boys.

Just as God knew it would.

A Gift from God

Mary Ann Cook

Where did you come from?" I asked the scraggly, tiger-striped kitten who had suddenly appeared on our doorstep.

"From God," answered my three-year-old son. "God took my cat, so he sent me one of his."

How else would you explain the cat's sudden appearance on the very day that Derrick's beloved cat had died? Coincidence? Maybe, but I preferred to look upon this kitten the way my son did—as a gift from God.

I carried the trembling kitten to the back patio where his plaintive meowing brought about the desired results. As the little kitten stood on wobbly legs, his head immersed in the creamy liquid set before him, Derrick giggled at the sight. The tears he had shed upon the loss of his pet were long gone, and he was relishing God's timely gift.

We named the kitten Morris because of his resemblance to the charming cat who pitched cat food on TV.

After his satisfying meal, young Morris napped in Derrick's lap. Suddenly a large tiger-striped cat appeared at the top of our rear embankment. Its loud, raspy cries awoke the kitten. He sat straight up and glanced toward the large cat. For a brief moment they stared at each other in silence. Then Morris plopped back down in Derrick's lap and closed his eyes.

The large cat cried out again. It became obvious that this was Morris's mother. It was also clear that she was telling him to hightail it back home. The wayward kitten didn't budge. His ears twitched ever so slightly but his eyes remained tightly shut.

The mother cat remained gazing at her kitten for a few minutes before climbing slowly back up the hill. I sighed in relief as she disappeared out of sight. My heart ached for this mother whose son had deserted her, but it would have ached even more had Morris followed her.

It was with a grateful and happy heart that I awoke the next morning to pour a bowl of kitten food for Morris. As he nibbled on the crunchy morsels, the mother cat appeared again. This time she bravely inched her way down the hill toward us. Her loud cries went unnoticed by Morris, who continued chowing down.

"Morris, I'm here!" Derrick shouted as he burst onto the patio. He scooped the kitten into his arms and stroked him tenderly before planting a kiss on his fuzzy, little head.

The mother cat ceased her crying but remained standing at the bottom of the embankment, a few feet from us. I wondered what was going through her mind as she watched the tender scene unfold before her. Would the sight of her kitten in the loving arms of my son be enough to reassure her that it was okay to relinquish him? I prayed that it would. As in answer to my plea, the mother cat took one long last look at her kitten. Then she turned and quietly made her way back up the hill. We never saw her again.

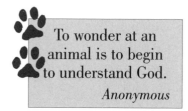

> To wonder at an animal is to begin to understand God.
>
> *Anonymous*

I hope she knows how much I appreciate the sacrifice she made that day. I like to think that she realized her kitten had found a good home with my son.

Watching that drama unfold between a loving mother cat and her tiny kitten, I could not help but think about a similar drama between a loving mother and her infant son some three years earlier.

I hope Derrick's biological mother knows how much I appreciate the sacrifice she made the day she gave him up for adoption. I like to think that she realized her son had found a good home with my husband and me.

A young boy and a young kitten—surely, both are gifts from God.

Three Cats and a Stepdad

Julianne Dwelle

Boots was my feline companion from my early teens until I moved out of the house at age eighteen. She helped me limp through adolescence. Best of all, she helped me connect to my distant stepfather—a connection that slowly but surely became as strong as blood.

But the story starts long before Boots came to our house.

When I was five years old, my mother brought home the man who would become my stepfather. He was a handsome, jovial fellow who winked at my sister and me and told us to call him Joe. His name was Hal.

I was craving a father at the time, and he seemed a likely character to fit the bill. Although I was a shy child, I talked to Hal and listened to his thrilling stories and liked him very much. Shortly after he married my mother, my sister and I talked it over and decided to call him Dad.

Now our single-mom household finally looked like a typical middle-class home of the late 1950s variety. My sister and I went to school down our country road, Mom stayed home and cooked and sewed, Dad went to work every day, then returned in the evening to his paper and a pre-dinner cigar. We even had a family dog.

But there was one wrinkle. Unfortunately Dad turned out to be a secretive guy with troubles he did not reveal to our mother. One evening after a couple of years of marriage, he did not come home. There were no fights in the house; he simply did not come home from work, and he stayed away for weeks.

My mother was beside herself with this unexpected problem in her marriage, but that's another story for another time. Let us just say that eventually Dad brought himself home with no real explanation. My mother took him back, and not much was ever said about it. In fact, the house became almost silent, and it would stay that way for years.

This silent, troubled household was a constant source of worry to me, a sensitive child. I found solace in my cat, a gray stray named Fluffy. She was a gorgeous, long-haired creature, and she bonded with me more than with the others in the house. She let me drape her over my shoulder and carry her everywhere. She slept on my bed every night. When she once gave birth to two stillborn kittens, she began birthing them on my bed. Fluffy and I were close.

I was ten years old when President John F. Kennedy was assassinated. I hurried home from school early that day, as did schoolchildren all over the frightened nation. At home, I found Fluffy sleeping in the middle of the living room floor and clearly not well. The country was in mourning all that weekend in a way we don't see today, and commerce shut down completely until after the funeral. That included veterinarians' offices. Since nobody in the farmland where I lived would ever have considered a sick cat an emergency, this meant we could not take Fluffy to the vet until after the president's funeral on Monday.

After the funeral, however, was too late, and Fluffy died at the vet's office the night after the president was laid to rest. The tension of the nation—and of my house—compounded my devastation.

That following spring, while walking home from school, I was approached by another long-haired gray cat right on the road. This cat looked so much like Fluffy that I did a double take. She appeared to be homeless. I'd never seen her before, and I was on a country road, so I assumed she was a drop-off. She simply walked out of a grassy ditch, gave a friendly meow, and rubbed on my ankles in that wonderful figure eight that cats do.

I petted the gray cat, and she followed me home. I truly believed God sent me this sweet and beautiful clone of Fluffy—I still believe that—to help me through my worries. I was tremendously grateful for her.

My mother gently asked me if I had "helped" the cat come home with me. But I was much too sensitive a child to have taken someone else's cat. Fluffy #2 really did appear on the side of the road and follow me home that day of her own volition, and she chose to stay.

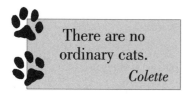

There are no ordinary cats.

Colette

The first Fluffy was a sweet creature, and this Fluffy was even sweeter. She, too, liked to be draped over my shoulder and carried everywhere. This Fluffy and our palomino gelding adored each other in a way I'd never seen between cat and horse. Whenever I wanted to ride but the horse didn't want to cooperate and be saddled, I would place Fluffy on my shoulder and walk into the grazing field. "Look who I have," I would coo to the horse.

The palomino would raise his head and saunter over to me. Fluffy purred while the horse nuzzled her. Then I would simply walk to the barn, the palomino following the purring Fluffy. I would plop Fluffy in the manger so the horse could nuzzle her some more, and the horse allowed himself to be saddled without so much as a whinny. Sometimes when he grazed, I would even lay Fluffy across his back, something that should have been dangerous. But the horse seemed to like it. He'd turn his head and nuzzle Fluffy—who purred the entire time—then go back to grazing.

Fluffy #2 and I had a couple of good years together. Then she disappeared one day and never returned. I was so inconsolable that at Christmas that year, my mother promised we would be intentional about finding another cat for me after the New Year.

During my short time with Fluffy #2, Dad walked out again. Like before, there was no fighting beforehand. He was gone for several weeks, then one day he just came home. Like before, my mother took him back. Again, nothing much was said. The house remained quiet.

As for me, I found the situation at home tense and unsettling. I ceased talking to my stepfather at all. He didn't speak to me either, really. In fact, for years, all we ever said to each other was along the lines of, "Please pass the milk." And I continued to worry over my silent household.

As a worried child, I did not sleep well. After that run of bad luck with the Fluffys, I rose before everyone else in the mornings to pore over the pet section of the classified ads, looking for another cat. Eventually I found an ad in which a woman wanted a home for what she called her "favorite cat."

Mom called the woman and learned that this cat needed more attention than the woman could give her because of her other house cats. When Mom told her that the cat would be for a twelve-year-old, the woman was not thrilled. She told my mother that this cat wasn't for children, and I heard my mother tell her, "My daughter is very mature for her age."

Apparently that was good enough. Or maybe it was hard to find a home for an adult cat of no particular breed that possessed a mighty strong will.

In any event, Mom and I drove to the lady's house that night, and we could see right away why Favorite Cat needed more attention. There were eighteen cats living in that small bungalow, and it was a sight I'd never seen before and never forgot. They were all hanging out in a cramped dining room, and the animal energy was noisy and intense. Cats vocalized and crawled all over the tops of tables and old-fashioned buffets, something that would never happen in my mother's house. It felt like we were interlopers in a miniature house of cats at the zoo.

Boots, already named, strolled into the room. She was a handsome, sturdy cat with round and expressive green eyes. Her short-haired coat was slate gray with white markings on her face and chest as well as on all her feet, creating perfect little boots. I would eventually learn that she had a strong personality—passionate, charming, and fierce. But at this first introduction, I simply noted her regal demeanor.

Boots must have caught on immediately that I was her ticket out of this feline Hades, because she looked me straight in the eye, then pranced to me and rubbed and rubbed on me and only me. This greatly impressed the woman, who remarked to my mother that Boots usually didn't like children. I suppose it could have been flattery, but the woman did seem genuinely surprised at the attention Boots gave me. I now wonder how many children had actually been inside the cat lady's house. At any rate, Boots became mine to take home.

Always Room for One More

Most cat behaviorists agree that a house needs one more litter box than the house has cats. If you have two cats, you can get away with two cat boxes, but one more is better. Why? Because bad cat behavior is usually closely linked to litter box issues. In multi-cat households, make sure that if one territorial cat commandeers one cat box (it happens), another box is available.

Keep litter boxes in private areas. And the most important thing you can do is scoop the boxes daily. There will never be odor in your home if you do.

Like the Fluffys before her, Boots slept on my bed every night and was a constant companion for me. Unlike the Fluffys, however, Boots was not what one would call sweet. She was not easygoing by any means, and she did not like to be draped over my shoulder or even picked up. She made that clear immediately—right after she whipped the family dog into some kind of canine she could live with.

But I adored Boots right away, and she seemed to like me well enough. I talked to her all the time, and she truly seemed to listen, her lovely white paws placed primly together as she looked into my eyes with a circumspect expression. This had not been the case with either Fluffy. I talked to Boots so much that one night I dreamed she could speak, too. Her voice was high and queenly and pitched like tiny bells. I asked her in the dream why she didn't ever talk before, and she laughed a sweet little laugh and did not answer; she simply looked mysterious.

I was privileged to be the person Boots slept with, and so this meant I was the one she woke up to get the day started. She did this by sitting on the bed stand and moving breakable items with her paw. The gentle scraping would wake me, and if I didn't get up, something would land on the floor—often my glasses. Of course I was annoyed, but looking back, I realize that it certainly beat alarm clocks.

And Boots had a way with Dad.

One morning during the early silent years before Boots, I had seen Dad feed a stray cat at the back door. We were always firmly instructed by my mother not to feed strays. Mom always had more pets than she really wanted, and they were almost never chosen, so she could be a little shrill about this stray thing.

But here was tense, noncommunicative Dad offering a bowl of milk to a stray cat at the door. And even better, he was speaking to it, softly and gently. I don't recall him ever talking to either Fluffy, so I wondered, *Is this really Dad?* In my world of stoic farmers and other hardworking men, I never saw any man pay positive attention to a cat. Never. To see the otherwise silent Dad paying such sweet attention to a cat . . . well, this knocked me out.

Dad raised his head and saw me. A look of guilt flashed momentarily across his face. "Don't tell your mother," was all he said. This was an interesting discovery for me, and now I knew that there was more to Dad than I had been seeing. I also noted that when it came to cats, Dad and I actually had something in common. I tucked the information in the back of my mind.

Consequently, it didn't take long after she moved in for Boots to discover the Inner Dad. Soon enough, she followed him around, prancing, purring, flirting, rubbing on his legs. And Dad liked it. He talked softly and gently to her. He talked more to Boots than he talked to any of the humans in the house. He even sang to her. He actually made up corny little tunes with her name in them, and, when he thought nobody was listening, he sang them to Boots.

In return, Boots sat with him while he had his early morning coffee by himself in the dark kitchen. She slept in his lap when he read the paper and on his clothes when he was away at work. And then Boots became a link between Dad and me.

How did she do that?

In a house where people don't speak, one can start believing they aren't listening either. I was listening to everyone, but I didn't know others were listening to me. But apparently Dad was at least listening to me speak to Boots.

the cat walks en pointe
skirting around my ankles
perfect figure eights

I tend to give nicknames to people and animals. So I sometimes called Boots other names, one being Mrs. Boogan. She was so stately that I felt she seemed like a Mrs. Somebody, and Mrs. Boogan is the name I came up with.

Pretty soon I heard Dad calling the cat Mrs. Boogan. After a while, that's all he called her. He even used her new name in his silly songs. Apparently he had listened to me sometimes.

This may not seem like a big deal, but I can't stress enough how we never spoke to each other. I felt invisible in my own home, and Boots seemed to make me visible again.

Boots also became a topic Dad and I could actually talk about to one another. When we sat at the silent supper table, sometimes Boots would hop up on an unoccupied chair and watch us. After a while, she would slowly extend one paw to the table. One of us would say in a mildly scolding tone, "Mrs. Boooo-gan. . . ." She would stop her paw midair and look around the table as if to say, "Is there a problem?" It was so delightful that we all relaxed. We teased her and fussed over her, and she loved the limelight. But it drew us together.

If we were away, the first thing Dad or I would ask about upon returning home was Boots. We both kept an eye out for her. We both talked to her. And sometimes, we talked to one another through her.

Eventually Dad and I would relax with one another. When I was old enough to drive, we relaxed even more, and I came to the conclusion that he was never comfortable with children. As I grew even older, we developed a bond. There came a day when we never lacked for something to talk about to one another.

Years later, my tough, silent stepfather wept openly at my wedding. And many years after that, at the time he lay dying in Florida, I was dreaming about him in Tennessee. He told my mother that I was in the room, next to him.

It took one strong-willed cat to kick-start a bond between two clueless humans. And it worked.

Acknowledgments

Many thanks to the talented and patient writers in this book who gave me the privilege of using their stories.

Many more thanks to the wonderful people at Revell and the rest of Baker Publishing Group who worked hard to make this book a reality.

Notes

1. Brian Sibley, *Through the Shadowlands: The Love Story of C. S. Lewis and Joy Davidman* (Grand Rapids: Revell, 1994; previously published 1985 in the UK by Hodder and Stoughton), 104.

2. "Dear Tabby," *Cat Fancy* (September 2003), 7.

3. Sibley, *Through the Shadowlands*, 172.

4. Robert Hudson and Shelley Townsend, *The Animal Muse* (Grand Rapids: Perciphery Press, 1988), 4. Used by permission.

5. Ibid., 6.

6. Karen S. Phillips VMD, "Indoor Versus Outdoor Living," *Cat Fancy* (August 2003), 54.

Contributors

Marci Alborghetti is the author of nine books, including *Twelve Strong Women of God* and *The Jesus Women*, two volumes of short fiction featuring women of the Bible; *The Miracle of the Myrrh*, an illustrated family Christmas book; and her latest, *How to Pray When You Think You Can't*. She has also contributed to *Daily Guideposts* and the *Chicken Soup for the Soul* books. She and her husband, Charlie Duffy, divide their time between Connecticut and Northern California.

Twila Bennett is the senior marketing director for a book publisher. Her stories have been published in *MomSense* magazine and in several books. She and her husband, Dan, enjoy their bright red speedboat every summer on Michigan lakes with their son, Zach. Every night, she cuddles with her spoiled dog, Tyson—a boxer who never listens to a word she says but whom she completely adores.

Robert Benson and the Monk live in Nashville, Tennessee. He is the author of more than ten critically acclaimed books, the most recent being *Digging In: Tending to Life in Your Own Backyard*. The Monk sleeps during the day, does not have a web address, and will not come even if you call her by name.

Sue Buchanan prefers to call herself a cheerleader rather than an author as she encourages her readers to "shake off the nay-sayers, break out of the mold, and embrace your authentic self." Her most recent book (number fourteen) is *The Bigger the Hair, the Closer to God: Unleashing the Cute, Darlin', Witty, Intelligent, Passionate, Authentic, Interesting, Life-of-the-Party Person Inside You!* Her award-winning children's books include *I Love You This Much* and *Dear God, It's Me*.

Renie Burghardt, who was born in Hungary, is a freelance writer. Her stories have appeared in anthologies and magazines, including *Chicken Soup for the Soul, Cup of Comfort, Guideposts*, and many others. She lives in the country and loves nature and animals.

Terri Castillo-Chapin is a former senior book editor with Guideposts Books. She is on a lengthy sabbatical and can be found these days traveling the world. She is the executive director of Akasha, Inc., a nonprofit corporation that preserves the musical legacy of her late husband, Thomas Chapin. She lives in New York City.

Linda S. Clare is the author or coauthor of three books, including *Making Peace with a Dangerous God*. She has won several fiction awards, teaches college writing classes, and works as a mentor and editor in Eugene, Oregon. She and her husband of thirty years, Brad, have four adult children who rarely climb trees anymore, but Oliver still competes with pals Xena Warrior Kitty and Paladyne for the best spot in any sunny window.

Mary Ann Cook offers hope and help for retired couples through seminars and through her book, *Honey, I'm Home for Good!* She and her husband, Ken, reside in Colorado

Springs, Colorado, with a hyperactive black feline whom the grandchildren call "Pepper Cat."

Lonnie Hull DuPont is a poet and book editor living in rural Michigan. Her poetry can be read in dozens of periodicals and literary journals, and her work has been nominated for a Pushcart Prize. She is the author of *The Haiku Box*, and her haiku about cats are scattered throughout this book. She and her husband, Joe, are owned by two brilliant felines.

Julianne Dwelle is the pseudonym for a writer of nonfiction who adores animals of all kinds.

Gwen Ellis's cat, Dickens, is fourteen years old as of this writing and still healthy, as is Gwen. She finished a career in publishing and then moved to southern California where she started her own writing and editing business, Seaside Creative Services. Dickens and Gwen were joined a few years ago by a rascally tuxedo cat named Tiny Tim. Gwen wants readers to know that there is life after cancer and that God is good.

Callie Smith Grant is the author of several nonfiction books for young readers and adults as well as many animal-themed stories and poems, which can be seen in Guideposts anthologies and in magazines such as *Small Farmer's Journal*.

Bonnie Compton Hanson's story was a winner in the 2003 Obadiah Press contest. She is the author of several books for adults and children, including the Ponytail Girls series and award-winning Hattie series. She has published hundreds of articles and poems, many in *Chicken Soup for the Soul* products. She is also a speaker to women's groups and schools and leads writing seminars.

Paul Ingram is a freelance writer and editor, living in Grand Rapids, Michigan. He and his wife, Sheila, no longer have children at home, but they provide bed and board for their daughter's aged Tonkinese, Snickers, and their son's charcoal gray cat of uncertain breed, Gracie. A former newspaper editor and college journalism instructor, Paul now works primarily in religious book publishing. He is a ruling elder in the Presbyterian Church in America.

Gregory L. Jantz, PhD, is the founder and executive director of The Center for Counseling and Health Resources, Inc. with four locations in the Seattle, Washington, area. For over twenty years, The Center has provided hope, help, and a whole-person approach to healing for people with eating disorders as well as other life issues. Dr. Jantz is married to LaFon, and they have two sons, Gregg and Benjamin.

Alyce McSwain has been writing short stories all her life. In addition to that, she is a retired Minister of Christian Education in the United Methodist Church, and she worked in drug abuse prevention for several years. She has been married for thirty-seven years and has two adult children, Jennifer and Robert.

Tracie Peterson is a bestselling author of over seventy books. She teaches at writing workshops and women's retreats, and she enjoys living in Montana with her husband, Jim, son, Erik, mother, mother-in-law, two collies, and three cats.

Linda Shands is the award-winning author of nine books as well as multiple articles and poems. She lives in rural Oregon with her husband, two dogs, one horse, and of course Molly the cat.

B. J. Taylor is an award-winning author whose work has appeared in numerous *Chicken Soup for the Soul* books, John Gray's *Mars and Venus in Love, Romantic Homes, Guideposts*,

Lexus, Writer's Digest, and many others. Happily married, B. J. and her husband share their home with one dog and three cats. B. J. is now writing a book about Rex's canine quest to find just the right job.

Jeanette Thomason lives with The Great Gatsby, a great white hope of a cat, in Colorado Springs, Colorado. She's been a correspondent, reporter, photographer, and editor of newspapers in the Pacific Northwest, two national women's magazines, a website, and now is an editorial director for a book publisher.

Amy J. Tol is a freelance writer and author of *The Bride's Handbook: A Spiritual and Practical Guide to Planning Your Wedding.* She and her feline friend live in Holland, Michigan, with her husband, Brian, and their son, Noah.

Thora Wease has worked as a stand-up comedian, a clerk in a trauma center emergency room (think "Jerry" on *E.R.*) and every bizarre and low-paying job in between. She is a graduate of Aquinas College in Grand Rapids, Michigan, where she received a Master of Management, B.A. in English, creative writing minor, and theological studies certificate. She writes poetry, screenplays, and creative nonfiction with the help of her cat, Joseph, her faithful "mews."

Lisa-Anne Wooldridge makes her home in Redwood Shores, California, with her husband, Andrew, and children, Jesse, Ivy, and David Blaze. The family is owned by two tiger cats—Scout and Comet. Lisa-Anne works as an author, teacher, and speaker, as well as a home educator and keeper of the catnip.